JN495397

김승희 – 달걀 속의 生

Life Within an Egg

한국문학영역총서

Life Within an Egg

Translated by Kyung-Nyun Kim Richards & Steffen F. Richards

Copyright © by Kim Seung-hee
English Translation Copyright © 2004 by Kyung-nyun Kim Richards and Steffen F. Richards

The publication of this book was supported by a grant from Korea Literature Translation Institute.

All rights reserved. No part of this book may be reproduced, stored in a retrieval system, or transmitted in any form, or by any means, electronic, mechanical, photocopying, recording or otherwise, without prior permission from the publisher.

Library of Congress Cataloging-in-Publication Data
Kim, Sæung-hæui, 1952-
I want to hijack an airplane : selected poems of Kim Seung-hee / Kim Seung-hee ; translated from the Korean by Kyung-nyun Kim Richards, Steffen F. Richards.— 1st American ed.
p. cm.
Includes bibliographical references.
ISBN 1-931907-13-7 (pbk.)
1. Kim, Sæung-hæui, 1952—Translations into English. I. Richards, Kyungnyun K. II. Richards, Steffen F. III. Title.
PL992.415.S92R53 2004
895.7'14—dc22
2003028260

Homa & Sekey Books
3rd Floor, North Tower
Mack-Cali Center III
140 E. Ridgewood Avenue
Paramus, NJ 07652

Tel: 201-261-8810; 800-870-HOMA
Fax: 201-261-8890; 201-384-6055
Email: info@homabooks.com
Website: www.homabooks.com

Published by Dap Gae Books
#2F 469-1, Gunja-Dong, Gwangjin-Gu, 143-838, Seoul, Korea
Tel | 02) 463-0464, 02)469-0464, 02)498-0464 / Fax | 02)594-0464

English Translations of Korean Literature Series
Publisher : Jang, So-Nim

김승희 – 달걀 속의 生

Life Within an Egg

Poems by Kim Seung-Hee

Translated by Kyung-Nyun Kim Richards & Steffen F. Richards

도서출판 답게

역자 서문

김승희 시인은 1952년 3월 1일 전라남도 광주에서 태어났다. 그는 5남매 중의 첫째였다. 부친 김인곤 씨는 전라남도 도청의 공무원이었고 모친 정경미 여사는 교사였다. 가정은 비교적 편안한 중산층이었으며 김승희는 별로 어려움 없는 가정 환경에서 자라났다. 부친은 엄한 편이었고 자녀들의 교육에 대하여 엄격했다. 그러나 모친은 낭만적이었고 자신이 책과 음악을 사랑한 정서적인 면을 가지고 있었다. 김승희는 유년시절부터 부모님의 이 두 가지 서로 다른 영향 속에서 자라났다.[1)]

광주에서 중학교를 마친 후, 김승희는 가족들과 함께 서울로 옮기게 되었으며 숙명여고를 거쳐 서강대학교에 입학했다. 1973년 서강대학교 영문과 3학년 재학 중, 그는 경향신문 신춘문예에 입선하여 시 부문에서 일등으로 입상하였다. 그의 문단 데뷔는 이렇게 이루어졌으며 그 당시 입상 작품은 「그림 속의 물」이었다.

1973년 등단이래 김승희는 단행본 시집 8권, 수필집, 이상평전, 그리고 두 권의 산문집을 출간했다. 작가로서 또한 교수로서 그는 여러 가지 수상경력을 가지고 있으며 1990년에는 이름 높은 소월시상의 영예를 안기도 했다. 그의 작품은 여성의 삶, 냉혹하고 비인간화되어 가는 도시 소시민의 생활, 그리고 절대적인 자유에의 갈망 등을 다루고 있다. 그의 시적 이미지는 어둡고, 강렬하며 때로는 매우 이례적이다. 그의 시에 많이 등장하는 색깔은 주로 빨간색인데 그것은 피와 불, 그리고 꽃의 색깔로 나타난다. 그의 시 세계에서 "불"은 예술적 열정과 힘을 나타낸다.

> 가로등이 다 꺼진 어둠 속으로
> 솜처럼 착하게 다 적셔져서
> 세상에서 가장 아름답게 타오르는
> 하나의 봉화가 되고 싶은지도 모른다.
>
> 「하나를 위하여」 부분

반면에 "꽃"은 예술적 성취의 미학적 형상의 상징으로 나타나고 있다.

> 어떤 고통은 토착의 형식으로만 꽃피어난다고
> 하는 전설이
> 그리고 나의 등에서 너울너울 꽃피어 타오르는
> 아네모네 둥근 뿌리의 찔러드는 파고듦을.
>
> 「아네모네 꽃이 핀날부터 · 4」 부분

"피"는 우리를 운명으로 엮어주는 인간관계의 상징으로 나타난다.

> 이 무슨 원한의 달콤한
> 피냄새—
>
> 「어머니가 나에게 가르쳐 주신 말」 부분

김승희의 작품은 치열한 지성과 감상에 접근하는 서정성의 독특한 융합이라고 할 수 있다. 그는 젊은 시절 니체와 카프카를 탐독했으며 그들의 철학적 사고에 매혹되었었다. 그는 작크 라캉, 미셸 푸코, 자크 데리다, 질 들뢰즈, 휠릭스 과따리, 롤랑 바르트, 그리고 최근에는 줄리아 크리스테바 등의 글을 탐독한다. 1990년대 풀브라이트 교환교수로 U.C. 버클리와 U.C. 어바인을 방문했을 때는 미국의 작가 에이드리엔 리치, 에리가 종, 마야 안젤루, 그리고 리타 더브 등의 작품을 애독했다. 특히 흑인 작가들인 마야 안젤루와 리타 더브의 작품에 동감을 느꼈는데 그것은 자신도 한국사회에서 일종의 소수그룹에 속하는 소외된 이방인이라고 느꼈기 때문이다.

1996년 U.C. 버클리에서 시 낭독회를 가졌다. 그때 그는 자신의 시 세계에 대해 다음과 같은 소개를 했다.

> 나는 쓴다. 나에게 제공된 세상만으로는 충분치 않기 때문에. 라 독사의 세계, 제도들의 세계, 당연한 것들을 믿는 것이 당연히 자연스러운 당연의 세계와 그것에 아무 반성 없이 동의하는 물론의 세계가 싫어서 나는 쓴다. 당연의 세계와 물론의 세계에 대한 거부.
>
> 연약한 달걀을 억압하는 냉혹한 힘 (달걀속의 생), 해방의 꿈은 너무도 현실적이고, 제도적이며, 막강하다. 달걀의 꿈을 억압하는 사회적, 정치적, 관습적인 힘은 고통스럽기 때문에 시를 쓴다. 자유와 평화를 추구하기 위해서는 아나키스트 달걀이 되어야 한다.

그래서 「세상에서 가장 무거운 싸움」은 당연과 물론의 세계에 길들여져 있는 나 자신과의 싸움이기도 하다. 당연의 속박을 풀기 위해서는 참으로 순결하고 힘찬 야성이 요청된다는 것을 느낀다. 활활 타오르는 상처의 꽃에서 훨훨 날아가는 새의 날개의 푸드득 솟구쳐 오름을 느꼈을 때…… 미소지었던 적이 있다. 나의 시가 그런 웃기면서도 엄숙한 어둠의 축제가 되었으면.

작 품

30년을 넘게 문학활동을 해 온 김승희 시인의 작품들을 정당히 논하자면 아마도 한 권의 책으로도 충분하지 못할 것이다. 이 번역본을 위하여는 매우 간략한 소개를 할 수밖에 없다.

그의 첫 시집, 『태양미사』는 1979년에 출간되었다. 시인 자신이 묘사하듯이 그의 "낭만주의"는 생명력의 성스러움으로부터 시작된다. 그리고 이 생명력은 불과 빛, 태양의 에너지로부터 시작된다. 그녀는 태양을 향하여 미사를 집전하는 동정녀의 역할을 맡는다. 이 번역선집의 처음 두 편의 시는 『태양미사』에 발표되었던 시들이다.

1983년에 출판된 그녀의 두 번째 시집은 『왼손을 위한 협주곡』이라는 제목을 달고 있다. 이 번역 시선에 수록된 시들은 다수가 이 시집에 수록된 시들이다. 여기에 수록된 시들은 다분히 여성을 주제로 한 것들이다. 「여인 등신불」은 분만실에서 벌어지는 여성의 고통과 새 생명 탄생의 승리를 생생하게 그리고 있다. 「배꼽을 위한 연가 1」과 「어머니가 가르쳐 주신 말」은 어머니와 딸의 분리될 수 없는 관계를 그리고 있다. 「만파식적」에서는 남편에게 질문을 던진다. "…더불어 살면서도 아닌 것 같이, 외따로 살면서도, 더불음 같이, 그렇게 사는 것이 가능할까?" 남편과의 사이에 투명한 빈자리가 놓이고 그 사이로는 바람이 흐르고 별들이 나부끼기를 제안한다. 그래서 현대 한국의 결혼하는 선남선녀들은 종종 결혼식에서 이 시를 마치 예전의 칼릴 지브란의 시를 낭송했던 것처럼 낭송하곤 한다.

『미완성을 위한 연가』는 1987년에 출판되었는데 이 시집에는 여성의 삶의 비참함을 그린 「곡비」와 기형적인 육체를 묘사하는 무용가를 위하여 쓴 시 「누가 나의 슬픔을 놀아주랴」등이 포함되어있다. 이 시들은 어둡고 슬픈 시임에는 틀림없지만 시인은 또한 그 여성들의 삶 속에 내재한 아름다움과 힘을 발견한다.

곡비는
장례의 가장 앞에 가고
무덤에서 가장 늦게 내려오는
실낙원의 도배사

「곡비」 부분

나는 병신입니다
우리는 병신입니다
이 슬픈 몸을 움직여
이 절뚝거리고 비비적대는
우스운 몸뚱아리를 움직여
한판 춤을 추다가

「누가 나의 슬픔을 놀아주랴」 부분

1989년 김승희는 『달걀 속의 생』이라는 시집을 출간했다. 이 책에는 같은 제목을 가진 시들이 시리즈로 나와 있다. 차거운 전천후 냉장고 속에 얌전히 정렬되어 있는 달걀은 냉혹하고 비인간적인 도시생활의 조건 속에 살고 있는 개인의 생활을 비유하고 있다. 이런 비유는 현대시의 시작법으로는 이례적일 수도 있지만 한국 고대의 전설 또는 신화를 보면, 많은 성스러운 인물들, 예를 들어 어떤 왕조의 첫째 왕 또는 시조가 알에서 나온 것임을 알 수 있다. 이런 각도에서 볼 때 알로부터 부화하는 생명의 가능성은 또 다른 차원의 의미를 갖게 된다.

탄생과 삶, 그리고 자유를 위하여 없어서는 안 될 따뜻한 보금자리에 대한 동경은 1990년대 김승희 시속에서 계속 전개되고 진화된다. 『어떻게 밖으로 나갈까』(1993), 『세상에서 가장 무거운 싸움』(1995) 등은 억압으로부터 벗어나는 개인의 변신과 해방을 주제로 한다. 모든 억압은 "제도"로 표상된다.

> 아이는 하루종일 색칠공부 책을 칠한다.
> 나비도 있고 꽃도 있고 구름도 있고
> 강물도 있다.
> 　　아이는 금 밖으로 자신의 색칠이 나갈까 봐 두려워
> 　　한다.
> 누가 그 두려움을 가르쳤을까?
> 금 밖으로 나가선 안된다는 것을
> 그는 어떻게 알았을까?
> 　　나비도 꽃도 구름도 강물도

모두 색칠하는 선에 갇혀 있다.

엄마, 엄마, 크레파스가 금 밖으로
나가면 안되지? 그렇지?
아이의 상냥한 눈동자엔 겁이 흐른다.
    온순하고 우아한 나의 아이는
    책머리의 지시대로 종일 금 안에서만 칠한다.

내가 엄마가 아니라면
나, 이렇게, 말해 버리겠어.
    금을 뭉개버려라. 랄라. 선 밖으로 북북 칠해라.
    나비도 강물도 구름도 꽃도 모두 폭발하는 것이다.
    살아 있는 것이다. 랄라.
    선 밖으로 꿈틀꿈틀 궁게뭉게 꽃피어나는 것이다
    위반하는 것이다. 범하는 것이다. 랄라

나 그토록 제도를 증오했건만
엄마는 제도다.
나를 묶었던 그것으로 너를 묶다니!
내가 그 여자이고 총독부다.
    엄마를 죽여라! 랄라.

「제도」 전문

평 론

김승희 시인은 흔히 이국적, 열정적, 그리고 야성적이라고들 평

한다.[1] 한 평론가는 김승희 시인을 가리켜 "늑대와 함께 달리는 여인"으로 표현했다.[2] 어떤 평론가는 김승희 시인을 가리켜 "아직도 부화(변신)의 꿈을 꾸는 시인, 하나의 아름다운 나비로 변신되기를, 하늘로 솟구쳐 오르는 자유로운 혼"이라고 보았다.[3] 현존하는 한국 시인 가운데 가장 관념적인 시인 중의 하나로도 평가된다. 김승희 시인은 포스트 모더니즘적 심리학과 철학에 매우 박학하며 그 학문적 지식을 자신의 작품에 반영시키고 있다. 그녀에게는 본연의 지성과 지적 추구가 매우 정교한 균형을 이루고 있음을 볼 수 있다.

김경년

Steffen F. Richards

2003년 8월

주 :

1) 김강태. 고독한 독립꾼, 야생마 김승희. 현대시. 1997년 8월호. 131-153쪽

2) 정효구. 늑대와 함께 달리는 여인. 세상에서 가장 무거운 싸움. 141-158쪽. 세계사 1995

3) 김성곤. 김승희 : 변신을 꿈꾸는 깨어진 영혼. 김승희 시 낭독회 강연. U.C. Berkeley. 1996년 11월 12일

Translator's Note

Kim Seung-Hee was born on March 1, 1952, in the City of Kwang-ju, Cholla-namdo Province. She was the first of five children born to the Kim family. Her father, Kim In-gon, was a civil service officer in the provincial office of Cholla-namdo, and her mother, Chung Kyung-mi, was a school teacher. The family led a relatively comfortable middle-class life and Kim Seung-Hee grew up in a carefree home environment. Her father was more strict and a disciplinarian in his approach to his children' s education, while her mother was more romantic and emotional through her own love of books and music. These two traits of her parents were a strong influence in Kim Seung-Hee's early years, and they still run deep in her life and work.[1)]

After the completion of her middle-school education in Kwang-ju, the family moved to Seoul where she attended Sook-myung Girls' High School and, later, Sogang University. While still a junior studying English literature at Sogang, she entered, in 1973, a literary contest held by *Kyung-hyang Daily News-paper*, and won first place in the poetry category. This brought about her formal recognition in the literary world in Korea. The title of her winning entry was "The River in the

Picture."

Since her official debut (1973), Kim Seung-Hee has published eight volumes of poetry, several collections of essays, a critical biography (of Yi Sang, based on her Ph.D. dissertation), and two novels. A prolific writer and a professor, she has won numerous honors and prizes, including the prestigious Sowol Poetry Award in 1990. Her works deal with the conditions of a woman's lot, the cold and dehumanizing aspects of modern urban life, and the longing for freedom as an absolute ideal. Her poetic imagery is dark, intense, and at times unconventional. The most characteristic color she uses is red, which appears in the images of blood, fire, and flowers. In her poetic world, fire stands for artistic passion and energy: *In the darkness, where no street lamps are lit, saturated like a piece of soft cotton, I might want to become a bonfire and burn ever so beautifully in the world!* (from "For the Sake of Being One"); while flowers stand for the glory of artistic achievement as the ultimate esthetic realization: *...the boring down of the bulbous anemone root into my back where flowers bloom and burn with dancing flames* (from "From the Day the Anemone Bloomed · 4") ; and blood for the human relations to which we are bound by destiny: *What is this sweet smell of blood, of my bitter resentment?!* (from "Words My Mother Taught Me").

Kim Seung-Hee's work is a unique blend of rigorous intellectualism and a lyricism that borders on the sentimental. In her youth she read voraciously and was fascinated by the philosophical thought of Nietzsche and Kafka. She is an expert on Jacques Lacan and avid reader of Michel Foucault, Jacques Derrida, Gilles Deleuze and Felix Guattari, Rolan Barthes, and, most recently, of everything written by Julia Kristeva. While visiting the University of California campuses at Berkeley and Irvine as a Fulbright scholar during the late nineties, she fell in love with certain American writers, such as Adrienne Rich, Erica Jong, Maya Angelou, and Rita Dove. She felt a special empathy for black women writers, like Angelou and Dove, as she has always felt herself to be a kind of minority and outsider in Korean society.

In 1996, when she gave a reading at UC Berkeley, she offered the following statement.

> *I write poetry because the world that is offered to me is not sufficient in itself. The world of La Doxa, the world of institutions, the world of "rightness" in which what is expected is naturally believed in and the world of "of course" that agrees with it without reflection; I write because I dislike such worlds. My act of writing is a refusal of the world of "rightness" and the world of "of course." ... The cold forces that oppress the fragile eggs'* [an allusion to a series of her poems] *dreams of liberation are all too realistic, institutional, and formidable as well. I write poetry because*

the social, political, and conventional forces that repress the dreams of eggs pain me. One has to become an anarchist egg in order to seek freedom and peace.... Therefore "the heaviest of struggles in the world" is the battle against myself, who am so well tamed in the world. I feel indeed that the purest and strongest untamed passion is necessary in order to unravel the bindings of "rightness." When I felt the burst of flight of a bird that soared up from the flames of wounds burning brightly, I smiled. I hope that my poems bring smiles and yet are a grave festival of darkness.

About Kim Seung-Hee' s Work

An adequate discussion on the work of a poet whose career spans thirty years and whose work comprises several volumes would require a book-length treatise. However, for the purpose of this volume, all that is required is a cursory look at her poetic writings.

Her first collection of poetry was published in 1979 with the title *A Mass for the Sun*. As the poet herself describes it, her "romanticism" stems from the sacredness of the life force, and this life force comes from fire and light, from the energy of the sun. She takes on the role of a virgin saying mass for the sun. The first two poems in the present (English) collection come from the first volume of her poems.

Published in 1983, her second collection was entitled *Concerto for the Left Hand*. Many of the poems contained in the present translation come from this volume and many of them deal with the theme of women. "Female Buddha" paints a vivid picture of a woman' s agony in the delivery room and the triumphant birth of a new life. "Love Song for the Belly Button 1" and "Words My Mother Taught Me" deal with the inseparable mother-daughter relationship. In "The legendary Flute of Shilla," Kim Seung-Hee poses a question to her husband, "Is it possible to live together, yet as if not, or to live apart, yet as if together?" She proposes that there be transparent space between husband and wife so that "a breeze could flow and stars could flutter through it." The poem is often recited at weddings of young couples in modern Korea, somewhat the way the writings of Kahlil Gibran have been used in the past.

Love Song for the Unfinished was published in 1987, which contains some very sad poems depicting a woman' s role as a hired "Wailer" at funeral processions and as a dancer depicting a grotesquely deformed body. While indeed these poems are dark and sad, the poet does see beauty and strength in these roles played by women.

The hired wailer walks
at the head of the funeral cortege

and leaves the gravesite
last:
the wallpaper hanger
of the lost paradise.
(From "Wailer")

I am deformed.
We are deformed.
Moving this sad body,
This limping and squirming,
Comical body,
I must dance a number before I go—
(From "Who Will Play with My Sorrow?")

In 1989, she published a collection entitled *Life Within an Egg*. A series of these poems have the same title "Life Within an Egg." The eggs, neatly lined up cold and frigid in the refrigerator, are used as a metaphor for individuals living in the cold and dehumanizing conditions of urban life. This metaphor might seem unusual as a modern poetic device, but if we look into the legends and mythology of ancient Korea, we find that numerous sacred personages, such as first kings of the founding fathers of dynasties, were born from eggs. When we take this into account, the possibility of life burgeoning out of eggs takes on a different and poignant dimension.

This yearning for the warmth of a nest, necessary for birth, life, and freedom, continues to evolve in her poems throughout the 1990s. *How Can I Get Out?*(1993) and *The Heaviest of Struggles in the World* (1995) deal with the transformation and liberation of the individual from everything that confines and oppresses. This is identified with institutions.

Institutions

A child colors in his coloring book all day long.
There are butterflies, flowers, clouds,
and also a river.
The child is afraid to color over the lines.
Who taught him this fear?
How did he come to know not to go over the lines?
The butterflies, the flowers, the clouds, and the river are all trapped
within the lines to the drawing.
Mommy! Mommy! The crayon shouldn't go over the lines, should it?
Fear flows across the tender eyes of the child.
My child, gentle and graceful, paints all day,
keeping within the lines according to the instructions at the front of the book.
If I weren't his mom,

I would have said:

The hell with the lines! La, la-la! Paint right over the lines!

Butterflies, rivers, clouds, flowers —let them explode!

They are living! La, la-la!

Beyond the lines, wriggling and rising, they bloom.

They defy. They violate. la, la-la!

I have so despised institutions,

and yet Mom is an institution.

I am the Governor General!

To think that I bind you with the very thing

that bound me!

Death to Mom! La, la-la!

What critics say about Kim Seung-Hee

Kim Seung-Hee is often considered exotic, passionate, and wild. One critic likened her to a "woman who runs with wolves."[2)] Another saw her as a dreamer of metamorphosis "who is still dreaming of hatching out, still dreaming of transforming herself into a beautiful butterfly, and still dreaming of soaring into the sky as a free spirit."[3)] She is also one of the most conceptually oriented poets among contemporary Korean writers. Her serious study into the psychological and philosophical developments of the post-modern era is well acknowledged and she makes use of her knowledge in her own creative work as well as in her critical essays and articles. In her, native intelligence and intellectual pursuit achieve an uncanny balance.

Kyung-Nyun Kim Richards
Steffen F. Richards
August, 2003

Notes:

1. Kim Kang-tae. *Lonely Independent Fighter, Wild Horse Kim Seung-Hee.* (In Korean) Hyun-dae Si. (Modern Korean Poetry). pp. 131-153. August 1997. Seoul, Korea
2. Jung Hyo-koo. *Woman Who Runs with Wolves.* The Heaviest of Struggles in the World. (Poems by Kim Seung-Hee) pp.141-158. (In Korean.) Se-gye-sa. Seoul, Korea. 1995
3. Kim Seong-kon. Kin Seung-Hee: *A Soul-wounded Dreamer of Metamorphosis.* Lecture delivered at UC Berkeley on the occasion of Poetry Reading by Kim Seung-Hee. Nov. 12, 1996

감사의 말

이 책을 번역 출간함에 있어 여러 개인과 기관에 힘입은 바가 크다. 한국의 *The Korea Times* 일간지는 처음 몇 편의 번역시를 높이 평가해 번역의 가능성을 인정하여 주었고 한국문예진흥원은 번역 지원금을 제공함으로써 작업을 가능토록 협조해 주었다. 샌프란시스코의 아시아 미술관의 문화 프로그램은 초기 번역 작품을 발표할 기회를 제공해 주었다. 산호세 주립대학의 김기청 교수, UCLA의 Peter Lee 교수, 서강대학의 안선재 교수, 그리고 U.C. Berkeley의 Robert Hass 교수 등은 초벌 번역과 여러 단계의 번역문들을 접하고 제안과 조언을 주었기에 여기에 감사하는 바이다. 물론 모든 부족한 점은 번역가의 몫임을 밝혀 둔다.

한국문학 번역원은 출판 지원 프로그램을 통하여 이 책의 출간을 가능케 하였으며 그에 대하여 심심한 사의를 표한다. Homa & Sekey 출판사의 편집 Shawn Ye가 보여준 집중력과 효율적인 작업, 그리고 인내심에 감사를 표하고 싶다.

마지막으로 영어권 독자들을 위해 번역 작업을 위임해 준 가장 중요한 사람, 원저자 김승희 시인에게 깊은 감사의 뜻을 전한다.

역자 김경년

Steffen F. Richards

2003년 12월 15일

Acknowledgments

IN TRANSLATING AND publishing this book, we owe much to many individuals and organizations. We want to thank The Korea Times of Seoul, Korea, for their first recognition of the possibility of this work, and the Korean Culture and Arts Foundation of the Republic of Korea for its generous grant in support of this translation project. We wish to express our appreciation to the Asian Art Museum of San Francisco for their cultural programs, through which the first poems were translated and read in public. Profs. Kichung Kim, Peter Lee, Bro. Anthony Teague, and Robert Hass, among others, have read drafts at various stages of the work and given valuable comments, suggestions, and constructive criticisms. However, any inadequacies or shortcomings are entirely our responsibility.

The Literature Translation Institute of Korea made the publication of this book possible through their publication-grant program and we wish to express our deep gratitude for it. To our editor, Shawn Ye, at Homa & Sekey, our big thanks are due for his focus, efficiency, and patience.

Lastly, we wish to thank the most important person of all, the poet, Kim Seung-Hee, for agreeing to let us translate her work and to bring it to the English-reading public.

Kyung-Nyun Kim Richards

Steffen F. Richards

December 12, 2003

차 례

Contents

미완성을 위한 연가
Love Song for the Unfinished

달걀 속의 生
Life Within an Egg

어떻게 밖으로 나갈까
How Can I Get Out

세상에서 가장 무거운 싸움
The Heaviest of Struggles in the World

태양미사

A Mass for the Sun

그림 속의 물

사랑스런 플란다스의 소년과 함께
벨지움의 들판에서
나는 예술의 말(馬)을 타고
알 수 없는 그림을 그리고 있었다.

그림은 손을 들어
내가 그린 그림의 얼굴을
찢고 또 찢고 울고 있었고.

나는 당황한 현대의 이마를 바로 잡으며
캔버스에
물빛 물감을 칠하고, 칠하고,

나의 미학 상식으로서는
그림은 아름답기만 하면 되었다.
그림은 거칠어서도 안 되고
또 주제 넘게 말을 해서도 안 되었다.

소년은 앞머리를 날리며
귀엽게, 귀엽게
나무다리를 깎고
그의 귀는 바람에 날리는

The Water in the Picture

With a lovely boy of Flanders,
in a field in Belgium,
I was painting some unknown picture,
riding on a horse of art.

The picture raised its hand
and again and again, tore the face in the picture I was
drawing, and it was crying.

Straightening the forehead of our flustered modern times,
I painted and painted the canvas
the color of water.

In my common sense of esthetics,
a picture need only be beautiful.
It ought not to be rough
or to speak presumptuously.

The boy, his bangs flying,
Was carving a wooden flute,
ever so adorably.
His ears were silver leaves

銀잎삭.
그는 내가 그리는 그림을 쳐다보며
하늘의 물감이 부족하다고,
화폭 아래에는
반드시 강이 흘러야하고
또 꽃을 길러야한다고 노래했다.

그는 나를 탓하지는 않았다.
현대의 고장난 수신기와 목마름.
그것이 어찌 내 죄일 것인가.
그러나 그것은 내 죄라고
소년은 조용히
칸나를 내밀며 말했다.

칸나위에 사과가 돋고
사과의 튼튼한 과육이
웬일인지 힘없이
툭, 하고 떨어지는 것이 보였다.
소년은 나에게 강을 그려달라고 부탁하였다.
강은 깊이깊이 흘러가
떨어진 사과를 붙이고
싹트고

blowing in the wind.
He looked at my picture and sang
that the sky lacked color;
that a river must flow
at the bottom of the picture,
and that I should grow flowers.

He did not blame me.
The broken receiver of modern times and the thirst—
how could they be my fault?
But they were my fault, the boy said quietly,
offering me a flower, a canna.
An apple shot out of the flower
and somehow the firm meat of the apple
could be seen dropping helplessly: plop!

The boy asked me to draw a river.
The river flowed deep
and attached the fallen apple;
buds came up,
flowers bloomed.
And in the picture a song arose

꽃피게 하였다.
그리고 그림엔 노래가 돋아나고
울려 퍼져
그것은 벨지움을 넘어
멀리멀리 아시아로까지 가는 게 보였다.

소년은 강을 불러
내 그림에 다시 들어가라고 말했다.
화폭 아래엔 강이 흐르고
금새 금새
훤한 이마의 꽃들이 웃으며 일어났다.

피어난 몇 송이 꽃대를 꺾어
나는 잃어버린 내 친구에게로 간다.
그리고 강이 되어
스며들어
친구가 그리는 그림
그곳을 꽃피우는 물이 되려고 한다.
물이 되어 친구의 꽃을 꽃피우고
그리고 우리의 죽은 그림들을 꽃피우는
넓고 따스한 바다가 되려고 한다.

and rang out
beyond Belgium
to a far, far-away Asia.
The boy summoned the river
into my picture again.
At the bottom of the canvas flowed a river
and swiftly, ever so swiftly,
flowers of bright foreheads rose up.

Picking a few stems of the flowers,
I run to my lost friend.
And I become a river
and seep into
the picture my friend is drawing
to become the water to make her picture bloom.
I want to become the water that makes my friend's flowers
    blossom
and to become the wide and warm sea
that brings to blossom our dead pictures.

태양미사

어둠이 태양을 선행하니까
태양은 어둠을 살해한다.
현실이 꿈을 선행하니까
그리고 꿈은 현실을 살해한다.
구름의 벽 뒤에서
이제는 태양을 산책하는 독수리여,
나는 감히
신비스런 미립자의 햇빛 파장이
나의 生을 태양에 연결시킬 것을
꿈꾸도다.
나의 生이 재떨이가 되지 않기 위하여
나의 生이 가면의 얼음집이
되지 않기 위하여
나는 감히 상상하도다.
영원한 궤도 위에서 나의 불이
태양으로 회귀하는 것을.
언제나, 그리고 영원토록.

나의 生命과 저 방대한 生命을
연결해 달라,
어떤 방직기계
어떤 안개의 無 속에서

A Mass for the Sun

As Darkness precedes the Sun,
the Sun slays Darkness.
Reality precedes Dream,
and Dream slays Reality.
Dear Eagle, who now promenades in the sun
behind a wall of clouds,
I dare to dream that
the mysterious particles of the solar rays
will join my life to the sun.
In order that my life not become an ashtray,
in order that my life not become
an icehouse of masks,
I dare to imagine
my fire, in perpetual orbit,
returning to the sun
for ever and eternity.

Please join
mine to that great life!
By what spinner of thread,
in what "nothingness" of a fog,
is our thread unwound?

우리의 실은 풀려지는 것인가?
어떤 증발
어떤 채무자인가, 우리들은?

나는 감히 상상하도다,
어둠이 태양을 선행하니까
그리하여 태양이 어둠을 살해하듯,
현실이 꿈을 선행하니까
그리하여 꿈이 현실을 살해하기를.
나는 감히
꿈꾸도다,
나의 生이 안개의 먹이로 환원되는 것을
나는 바라지 않기에
살기 위해 더 많이 사랑할 것을
오직 나는 바라기에
나는 감히 상상하도다,
영원의 궤도 위에서 나의 불이
태양으로 회귀하는 것을.
그리하여 존재의 실(絲)패를 태양에 감으며
신비스런 미립자의 햇빛 파장이
나의 生을 태양에 귀의시킬 것을.

What kind of vapor,
what kind of debtors are we?

I dare to imagine:
Darkness precedes the Sun,
therefore, the Sun slays Darkness;
since Reality precedes Dream
therefore, Dream should slay Reality.
I dare
to dream.
Because I do not wish
my life to return and become food for the fog,
and hope only that I will love more in order to live,
my fire returning to the sun
in perpetual orbit.
And so, by winding the spool of my existence around the sun,
the mysterious particles of the solar rays
will restore my life to the sun.

왼손을 위한 협주곡
Concerto for the Left Hand

태양의 면죄부

희디흰 폭양 속에선
어디선가 사물놀이패들 노는 소리,
징, 바라, 장고, 북—
징, 바라, 장고, 북—
어디엔가 원한의 무지개들 세우는 소리,
들립니다.

신비로워라,
삶의 무늬와 태양의 무늬가
어느 허공중에 가벼이 부딪쳐
저리도 찬란한
색채의 거울을 세움이여—

누가 내 몸속에 꼭꼭 채운 지푸라기들을
꺼내고
신을 가득 채우니—
오늘 같은 날은
언제나 원수 같았던 거울 속의 저 사람도
썩어가는 죄업으로 인해
더욱 진하게 보입니다
더욱 향기로워 보입니다

The Indulgences of the Sun

In the white heat of the sun can be heard
the sound of a farmer's band playing somewhere.
Small gongs and large, hourglass drums, large drums—
small gongs and large, hourglass drums, large drums—
The sound somewhere of putting up a rainbow of resentment
can be heard.

O, how marvelous!
Patterns of life and patterns of the sun
collide so lightly in the void,
setting up such a brilliant mirror of color!

Someone takes out all the straw packed
in my body
and fills it with the divine.
On a day like this,
even the one in the mirror who seemed the enemy,
appears more distinct,
more fragrant.

Someonc, please trim away every small branch of bone
and drill holes for a flute

내 뼈의 잔가지들을 훑어서
척추의 둥근 고리뼈를 중심으로
누가 피리 구멍을 내주세요.
오장 육부 굽이치는 원한의 강물에
입술을 대고
누가 저 목숨의 피리를 불어서
내 뼈를 신의 脈으로
가득 채워주세요.

호화로워라,
원한의 무늬와 폭양의 무늬가
어느 허공중에 진하게 부딪쳐
저리도 잔인한
뼈의 향유를 부음이여—

around the discs of my spine.

To the river water of suffering where the intestines wind,
place your lips
and play the flute of that life
and fill my bones
with the pulsing of a god.

How glorious!
The patterns of suffering and patterns of the sun
collide so intensely in the void
and pour out a perfumed oil of bone that is
so cruel.

남도唱

東녘은 많지만
나의 태양은 다만 무등 위에서 떠올라라

나는 남도의 딸,
문둥이처럼, 어차피, 난,
가난과 태양의 혼혈인걸,

만장 펄럭이는 꽃상여길 따라따라
넋을 잃고
망연자실 따라가다가
무등에 서서—
무등에 서서—

가난한 사람들의 얼굴 위에
妖花처럼
이글거리며 피어나던
붉은 해 덩어리를 보았더니라,
모두들 사당패가 되자 함인가,
백팔번뇌 이 땅을 용서하자 함인가,

신명 지펴 신명 피어
벌레 같은 한 평생

Song of the Southern Province

There's a great deal of sky in the east,
but the sun for me rises only above Moo-deung Mountain.

I am a daughter of the Southern Province.
Like a leper, without a choice, I am
but the mixed blood of poverty and the sun.

On the path of the flowered bier and fluttering banners,
I followed along, aimlessly,
losing my senses: and then
I found myself standing on Moo-deung Mountain;
I found myself standing on Moo-deung Mountain.

On the faces of the poverty-stricken
I had seen the red lump of the sun
bloom, flames rising like lurid flowers.
Do they all want to become migrant musicians?
Do they all wish to forgive this Land of the Hundred-and-
Eight Sufferings?

Entranced, and in a trance,
with lifetimes like those of insects,

가난도 아니고
죄도 아닌 사람들,

나는 남도의 딸,
징채잽이처럼, 어차피, 난,
가락과 신명의 혼혈인걸,

무등의 가락으로 해가 질 때만
노을은 원한이 되는 것이니—
천치도 아니고
부처도 아닌
내 고향 사람들의 울음을 모아
지는 해
굽이굽이
서러운 목청

돌아가— 돌아가서—
내 썩은 오장육부를 징채 삼아
한바탕 노을을 두들겨보노니
붉은 해 덩이는 業果처럼 둥글다가
문득 스러지면서
가장 진한 남도唱을

the people, who are not poverty itself,
the people, who are not sin itself.

I am a daughter of the Southern Province.
Like a gong player, without a choice, I am
the mixed blood of tune and trance.

Dusk becomes regret
when the sun sets to the melodies
of Moo-deung Mountain.
Neither idiots
nor buddhas,
the people of my hometown
raise their lamentations
to the setting sun,
their mournful voices
echoing in wave after wave.

I return, return to
make my rotten innards,
the Five Intestines and the Six Organs,
into a gong stick

철천지에— 뿌리더라—

and let loose, beating the dusk.
The red lump of the sun, rotund,
like the fruit of sin
suddenly receding,
scatters the most heart-wrenching
Southern song
into the sky.

난폭

운신할 기운조차 없다
꿈처럼 방이 무너져내리고
선반 위의 살림살이들이 쓰러져
내 몸을 붙들고
아프게 때린다

죽을 힘을 다해
나는 돌아눕는다
허공에서 거울이 깨어지며
나의 목아지를 병마개처럼 따고
한 송이 吊花를 꽂고 있다

순간 피는 손바닥으로 얼굴을 가리고
울기 시작한다
나의 골에선 찬란한 단두대의
밧줄이 뻗어나와
나의 목아지를 향해 달려 나간다

온몸이 찢기며
나는 웃는다
찬란한 미소가 뜨거운 찻물처럼
끼얹히는 것을 느끼며

Wanton Violence

I have no strength to move my body.
The room tumbles down as in a dream
and the things on the shelf fall off
and hit my body hard.

I turn in my bed
with all my might.
The mirror breaks in the void,
cutting my neck as if removing a bottle cap,
and sticking in a flower of condolence.

Momentarily, the blood on my palm covers my face
and I begin to cry.
From my skull, the rope of a dazzling guillotine
rushes out toward my neck.

As my entire body is being torn apart,
I laugh.
I feel a radiant smile being thrown over me
like hot tea;
my heart, however, assigns no blame.

나의 심장은, 그러나,
아무것도 원망하지 않는다

열파가 나의 두 눈을 감긴다
용암불에 성냥이 닿은 것처럼
나의 뼈 퉁소와 같은
나의 긴 뼈엔 향기로운 신이 가득하여
누에고치의 얇은 막처럼
가벼이 나의 피부가 터지는 것을
나는 알 수 있다

그렇게 죽어라
아니, 아니, 그렇게 삶을
맛보거라
삶이여— 너— 아름다운 흉성이여
기꺼운 치욕이여—

A heat wave closes my eyes.
As if a match has been thrown onto a flow of lava,
my bones, like flutes, my long bones
are filled with fragrant divinity.
I can feel my skin popping
like the cocoon of a silkworm.

Die that way!
No, no: live life that way!
Life...you...beautiful star of misfortune,
delightful humiliation....

몸속의 괴물이 뛰쳐나오려는 광인의 노래

울부짖는 입,
입을 목젖까지 환히 벌리고
거울 속을 들여다본다,
목젖을 밀치고
누군가가, 아니, 무엇인가가
힘껏 나오려고 한다,
털복숭이의 손이 보이고
털복숭이의 몸이 보이고
검은 장미꽃 이파리같이
뿌리칠 수 없는 눈동자가 보이고
보이는 것들은 무슨 엄청난 힘으로
오히려 입술을 잠궈버린다,

말해요—그것은 명한다,
말하라—그것은 다그친다,
말하세요—그것은 회유한다,
말해주세요—그것은 애걸한다.

자음과 모음과 구절과 문장들은
오장 육부 속에서 꾸룩거리고
아직 무지한 그것들은
온통 소리소리로 난장을 친다,

The Song of a Madwoman Whose Monster Is about to Leap from Her Body

My screaming mouth
wide open to reveal my uvula,
I peer, into the mirror.
Someone, or rather Something,
is trying with all its might
to come out and push through my uvula.
I see the hand of a hairy monster,
and the body,
and an irresistible eye,
like the petal of a black rose.
Everything visible seals my lips
with tremendous power.

Speak! Please!—it ordains.
Speak!—it urges.
Please speak!—it cajoles.
Please speak for me!—it begs.

The consonants and vowels, phrases and sentences
rumble in my intestines
and being ignorant
create chaos with scream after scream.

어떤 죄업을 씻기 위해
피 묻은 입들,
나는 조용히 미쳐간다,
배고픈 눈동자에 누군가 자꾸 바늘을
꽂는다……

My lips bloodied to cleanse away my sins,
I go mad silently.
Someone is pushing needles
into my hungry eyes....

시인의 노래

그대에게, 나는, 나의 말을 주고 싶다,
괴로움 한결 가득하여 찢어진 얼굴들,
우왕좌왕 번뇌와
갈팡질팡 희망에게,
말 못하는 짐승과 어린것들에게
나는, 모조리, 나의 말을 주고 싶다,

나의 말을 주기 위하여
그대여, 나는 너를 죽이지 않으면 안 된다,
하나의 풍각쟁이가
세상이 끝난 어느 날
매몰의 유적지에서 하나하나
실신한 사체들을 불러
일으키는 것처럼,

그대에게, 나는, 도형수가 되어야 한다,
그냥 있는 꽃의 아름다움과
그냥 있는 슬픔의 지느러미가
아무리 귀하고 선연한 것이어도
나와는, 결코, 아무 상관 없는 것,

그대에게 나는 나의 넋을 주고 싶다.

Song of a Poet

To you, I... I want to give my words:
you with your faces lacerated, full of constant suffering;
you, the troubled in your wanderings;
you, the hopeful in your indecisiveness,
you, you speechless animals and you young:
to you, altogether, I wish to give my words.

To be able to give you my words,
dear You, I must kill you.
Like a musician who,
on the day the world ends,
calls up the corpses that have lost consciousness
from their burial sites, one by one,
to you I have to be an executioner.

The beauty of flowers in their natural state
and the fish fins of sorrow the way they are
no matter how precious, how clear they may be,
to me, they never mean anything.

To you I wish to give my soul.
If the people of Abhasvara*

입을 열면, 그냥, 그대로,
빛이 쏟아져 나온다는
光音天의 사람들,

내가 파괴한 시체의 門을 열고
나는, 고스란히, 나의 피를 주고 싶다,
그리하여
어떤 깡패가 발길로 걷어찬
밥상 같은 만물에게
나는, 고요히, 내 피의 문맥을 부여하고 싶은
것이다

just opened their mouths,
light would stream out,
just like that.

Opening the door to the corpses that I destroyed
I... wish to give my blood, all of it, and
so, to all things that resemble
a table kicked in by a hoodlum,
I, serenely, wish to bequeath the pulsing of my sentences
written in blood.

---

*Abhasvara: (Sanskrit) The third of the three heavens comprising the second group of the dhyana heavens in the rupadhatu. There rays of light are emitted from the mouth and turn into words. Tr.

유서를 쓰며

내 뼈에 가득 찬
죄악을 비우기 위하여
나는 유서를 씁니다.
독한 청산가리 같은 잉크에
내 넋의 붓을 적셔
한 자 한 자 공들여 적어봅니다.

선언합니다.
내 몸의 모든 세포들에게,
시시한 추억들,
못 잊을 가족들에게
이것저것 유품을 나누어 놓고
이것이 최후라고
단호히 선언합니다.

그리고 부엌으로 들어가
문틈을 샅샅이 레이스로 봉합니다.
그리고 가스 마개를 틀고
더러운 부엌 바닥에
냉정히 드러눕습니다.

그리고 아직 너무나 젊기에
더 살고 싶다는 푸르른 나의 육신에

Writing a Will

To empty out the sins
which fill my bones,
I am writing a will.
I write each character with care,
dipping the brush, my soul,
into the ink, toxic potassium cyanide.

Distributing
to all the cells of my body
my trivial remembrances, and
to all my unforgettable family members
the knick-knacks of my belongings,
I declare this to be the last.
I declare it decisively.

I enter the kitchen
and seal the doors with lace;
turn on the propane
and coolly lie down
on the dirty kitchen floor.

I hammer a few nails
into my young body, still so green

못을 탕—탕—박고
망치를 허공으로 던져버립니다,
살점이 튀고
아까운 피가 양수처럼 따뜻이 고입니다,

이제야 생각납니다.
기역—니은—디귿! —하고
어머님께 매를 맞으면서
처음 글씨를 배웠던 일이,
첫애를 낳을 때의
그 무시한 고통과
현란을 극한 사랑의 고마움이,

번개처럼 일어나
창문을 열어봅니다,
달빛이 初雪처럼 흘러내립니다,
나의 해골을 집어 들고
달빛을 한 바가지 가득 떠서 마십니다,
고해를 하고 성찬을 받은 것처럼
목숨이 더없이 맑아진 것 같습니다.

and longing to live,
and toss the hammer into the void.
Pieces of my flesh jump
and precious blood warmly collects
like amniotic fluid.

Now I remember:
the first time I learned,
my mother using a whip,
to write ki-yok, ni-un, and ti-geut;*
and the terrifying pain and
gratitude for the most dazzling love
I felt at the birth of my first child.

I get up like lightning
and throw open the window.
Moonlight comes streaming down like a first snow.
I pick up my skull and
fill it with moonlight and drink.
My life seems much clearer,
as if I have received Holy Communion
after confession

* The first three letters of Han-geul, the Korean alphabet. Tr.

공포 영화

나는 언제나 쫓기고 있지,
공포 영화 속의 주인공 배우처럼
나는 끝까지 쫓기고 있지,
막연한 액운의 별 아래
영문 모르고 살다가
어느 날 갑자기 쫓기기 시작한다는
진부한 줄거리로
지치지도 않고 계속 돌아가는
오늘도, 잠 속의 낡은 영사기……

이제 자막에서 비는 내리고
비를 맞으며
하염없이 쫓겨가는 희미한 뒷모습……
무슨 범죄를 저질렀을까?
무성의 자막 위에
암호처럼 쏟아지는 희미한 외국어들,
왜 범인이 되었을까?
의문마저도 잊어버린 정박의 꽃처럼
온통 사위엔 쫓겨가는 움직임뿐……

바라건대 악몽은 악몽일지라도
한평생 깨지 않는 악몽이라면

Horror Movie

I am always being chased.
Like the leading actor in a horror movie,
I get chased until the end.
With the tired ol' theme of
someone who, so unaware of things and
under some vague star of ill fate,
suddenly one day begins to be chased—
the old projector in my sleep, again today,
continues to roll unwearied.

Now rain is falling from the subtitles,
and under the rain
the faint rear-view of someone being endlessly chased....
What crime could he have committed?
Over the silent subtitles,
faint foreign languages pour down like secret codes.
How did he become the culprit?
Like an anchored flower which forgot even the question itself,
there is nothing but the movement of being chased....

All I care about is, nightmare or not,
I do not wake from it as long as I live.

그건 좋은 거야,
그건 오케이야—
오, 그런데, 나는 참 찬란한 애정 영화가
한 편 보고 싶다,
그리고 무섭도록 사치스런 예술 영화도
한 편……

That would be good!

That would be O.K.!!

Oh, by the way, what I really want to see is a dazzling,

romantic movie,

and a horrifyingly luxurious art film,

too....

여인 등신불
—세브란스 병원 분만실에서

한 남자를 사랑했다고 하여
이런 고통이 있는 것은 아닙니다
한 남자와 잠깐 쾌락을 같이 했다 하여
이런 원통한 아픔이
있는 것은 아닙니다
여인들이여, 울고 찢기고 흐느끼며 발광하는
여인들이여,
이 성스러운 하얀 굴속에서
한 남자란 지극히 사소한 우연에
지나지 않습니다
짐승처럼 짐승처럼 지금 우리가
온몸을 물어뜯으며 울부짖는 것은
스님이 영혼을 구하기 위하여
다비의 불바다 속으로 들어감과 같습니다
하얀 도자기를 구워내기 위하여
불가마 속에 천하무비의 큰 불을
지피는 것과 같습니다

도살장에서 젊은 도수가 하염없이
나의 정수리에 도끼를 내려치는
것 같습니다
도끼날이 나의 숨골에 박힐 때마다

Female Buddha

—In the delivery room of Severance Hospital

It is not because I loved a man
that I suffer this way.
It is not because I shared a moment of pleasure with a man
that I have such excruciating pain.
Oh, women!
Women, you who cry, torn apart, who sob and flail!
In this sacred white cave,
man is no more than an accident
of the utmost triviality.
Like a beast, a beast, we bite at our whole body
and scream—
like a Buddhist monk entering Jhapita,* the sea of flames,
in order to save his soul;

or like setting sparks to the greatest pyre inside a kiln
in order to fire the whitest porcelain.

I feel as if a young butcher in the slaughterhouse is beating
the top of my skull with an ax,
with no end to it.
Each time the blade hacks into my soft spot,
petals of white flame spark up endlessly

흰 불의 꽃송이가 하염없이 튀어올라
흩어지고 있습니다
만다라의 꽃잎입니다
자비의 세례입니다

그대—죄가 있었으면
죄를 태우십시오
그대—업이 남았으며
업을 태우십시오

여인들의 울부짖는 소리가 어찌
범패보다 아름답지 않습니까?
범패보다 더 진한 막다른 소리들이
관처럼 하얀 방을 자욱이 메웁니다
오뇌와 비원의 처절한 촉수들이
찢어지는 살점을 쥐고 흔듭니다

쾌락처럼 그렇게 실신하면서
나는 천지 아득히 터지는 범종 소리를
들은 것 같습니다
아가의 울음소리—갓난둥이의 첫울음소리가
문득 하나의 太虛를 울리고

and scatter.

The petals of a mandala.

The baptism of compassion

If you... had sins,

burn those sins.

If you... have any karma left,

burn that karma.

Why is the sound of a woman screaming

any less beautiful than that of a Buddhist chanting?

Primal sounds more intense than a Buddhist's chants

thickly fill the room, white as a coffin.

Desperate tentacles of suffering and misery

grab hold of tearing flesh to shake it.

Losing my mind as though in ecstasy,

I seem to have heard the breaking

of a temple bell in a distant universe.

The sound of a baby's cry...the first cry of a newborn infant

is suddenly ringing in the great void,

and a blob of blood, heroic as a prophet,

신탁처럼 장렬한 핏덩이 하나가
이제 삶 속에 우뚝 섭니다
우리는 어디에서 와서 어디로 가는가—
하얀 잠이 가득히 와서
내 육체의 모든 문을 꼭꼭 여며주고 있습니다

stands bravely in the midst of life.

Where do we come from, and where do we go...?

White sleep fills me completely

and closes all the doors of my body tight.

---

* (Sanskrit) Funeral pyre. Tr.

배꼽을 위한 연가 · 1

그대여, 당신이 누구든지 간에, 당신의 배꼽을 보여준다면, 나 그대를 사랑하겠습니다, 더럽게 뒤엉긴 자그만 동그람이 굽이굽이 꼬불쳐진 그대의 서러운 배꼽도 나의 배꼽과 똑같이 부끄러운 죄와 어리석은 욕망이 고불고불 서리서리 끼어 있을 테지요, 그대여, 어둠의 태 속에서 영문 모르고 튀어나와 정처없이 죄를 짓고 죽어가는 그대여, 그대여,

우리는 배꼽 위에서 평등하다
그것은 생일날의 흉터,
고아들의 패찰,
인광을 칠한 백골의 주황색 입술이
아삭아삭 제일 먼저 뜯어먹는
온순한 육체의 이삭,
우리는 배꼽 위에서 너무나 평등하다

그대여, 당신이 누구든지 간에, 당신의 배꼽을 버리지만 않았다며는, 나 그대를 열렬히 용서하겠습니다, 봄이 되어 메마른 나뭇가지에서 새싹이 트는 것을 바라보거나 푸드득— 새들이 날아오르는 것을 볼 때마다 나는 습진처럼 나의 배꼽이 가려워지는 것을 느낍니다, 이제 배꼽은 과거 완료가 아니라 언제나 현재 진행형으로 나의 삶속에 움터 오르고, 어머니— 아, 어머니—라고 불러보면 바닷가를 울면서 걸어가는 한 여인이 떠오릅니다, 그녀

Love Song for the Belly Button · 1

Dear You, whoever you are, if you show me your belly button, I will love you. A small circle caked with dirt, all wound up, your sad little belly button—just like mine—is filled with shameful sin and silly desires, in every nook and cranny. Dear You, you who were expelled from the womb of darkness, who aimlessly commit sin and die. Oh, You!

We are equal in our belly buttons.
They are the scars of our birthdays, the name tags of orphans,
 the gentle grass of our flesh,
the vermilion lips of the white skeleton painted with phosphate
 bite first.
We are so equal in our belly buttons.

Dear You, whoever you are, if you have not abandoned your belly button, I heartily forgive you. When I see, in the springtime, new shoots budding on barren branches, when I see birds spring suddenly into the air, I feel my belly button itching as if with eczema. And now my belly button is not in the past-perfect tense, but it is budding, as always, in the present-progressive of my life. And Mother... ah, Mother... as I say this, I recall a woman walking along the beach, weeping.

의 슬픔 그녀의 사랑 그녀의 절망을 따라 나의 배꼽은 또 하염없이 시원의 태 속으로 적셔 들어가고, 어머니— 자비와 저주의 비밀 계좌이신 어머니—나의 어머니시여……

Pursuing her sorrow, her love, and her despair, my belly button enters the womb at the beginning of time. Mother!... Mother! My secret entry into compassion and damnation... My dear Mother...!

배꼽을 위한 연가 · 2

어머니가 말이 없으면
나는 무서워집니다
어머니는 우울한 것 같습니다
무섭게 불행한 것 같습니다

말이 없는 어머니보다는
잔소리를 하는 어머니가 더 좋습니다
싫은 소리를 하더라도
몇 마디 말을 하는 어머니가
덜 우울한 것 같아서
어머니—하고 치마폭을 붙잡고
달려가 어리광을 부리고 싶어집니다

그러나 제일 좋은 것은
등꽃나무 아래 평상을 내놓고 앉아
어머니가 완두콩을 까면서
느릿느릿 노래를 부르실 때입니다
어머니의 노랫소리는
뉘엿뉘엿 지나가는 해를 붙잡아
우리집 꽃밭에 옥잠화처럼 앉혀 놓는 것 같습니다
그런 때는 어머니가 행복하신 것이라고
나는 생각했습니다

Love Song for the Belly Button · 2

When Mother doesn't say anything,
I get scared.
She seems depressed,
terribly unhappy.

I prefer Mother's nagging
to her silence.
Even were she to say something I wouldn't want to hear,
it would be better, for she is less depressed when she talks.
I feel like running up to her, clinging to her skirt,
and becoming a child.

The best time is
when she sings slowly
as she shells peas,
sitting on the bamboo cot under the wisteria.
Mother's singing
catches the slowly setting sun
and plants it in the flower garden, like plantain lilies.
At such times, I thought, she was happy.

I went to the circus

어머니의 손을 잡고
서커스단 구경을 갔습니다
공중 곡예를 하는 어린 소녀가 줄을 놓고
잠시 허공에 떠 있다가
가벼이 그네를 박차며, 마치 전류처럼,
소녀의 손을 붙잡을 때
어머니는 아편을 마신 듯이 황홀하신 것 같습니다
어머니의 검은 눈동자 속엔 신비한
스파크가 떨며 지나갔습니다

이제 어머니는 말하지 않습니다
잔소리도 하지 않고
푸른 완두콩도 까지 않습니다
나는 어머니의 막혀버린 노래가
어느 날, 지진처럼, 발광하지 않을까—
겁이 납니다
어머니의 얼굴은 점점 슬픔의 얼굴처럼
굳어갑니다

holding Mother's hand.
At one point, the trapeze artist, a young girl, let go of her
  ropes,
floated for a moment in midair,
kicked the swing away, and, as if by an electric current,
caught the boy's hands:
Mother seemed in ecstasy as though she had been smoking
  opium.
Mysterious sparks passed through her dark eyes, trembling.

Now Mother does not speak.
Neither does she nag
or shell green peas.
I am afraid that
someday the songs Mother has stopped singing
will explode, with the effect of an earthquake.
Her face has become rigid,
a face of sorrow.

배꼽을 위한 연가 · 5

인당수에 빠질 수는 없습니다
어머니,
저는 살아서 시를 짓겠습니다

공양미 삼백 석을 구하지 못하여
당신이 평생 어둡더라도
결코 인당수에 빠지지는 않겠습니다
어머니,
저는 여기 남아 책을 보겠습니다

나비여,
나비여,
애벌레가 나비로 날기 위하여
누에고치를 버리는 것이
죄입니까?
하나의 알이 새가 되기 위하여
껍질을 부수는 것이
죄일까요?
그대신 점자책을 사드리겠습니다
어머니,
점자 읽는 법도 가르쳐드리지요

Love Song for the Belly Button · 5

Mother,
I can't jump into the Indang Sea;*
I have to live and write poetry.

Even if you had to remain blind your whole life
because I could not get the three-hundred sacks of rice to
   offer
Buddha,
I would never jump into the Indang Sea.
Mother,
I want to stay here and read my books.

Dear Butterfly,
My dear Butterfly,
Is it a sin for a little worm to shed its cocoon
so that it might fly as a butterfly?
Would it be a sin for an egg to break
so that a bird might emerge?

I will buy you books in Braille, instead,
Mother,
and I will teach you Braille that you might read them.

우리의 삶은 모두 이와 같습니다
우리들 각자가 배우지 않으면 안 되는
외국어와 같은 것—
어디에도 인당수는 없습니다.
어머니,
우리는 스스로 눈을 떠야 합니다

Our lives are all like this,
a foreign language
that each one of us has to learn.
There is no Indang Sea anywhere,
Mother:
we all have to open our eyes by ourselves.

---

* The sea in which Shim Chong (whose story is told as part of the traditional P'ansori repertory) was sacrificed as a peace offering. She was the filial daughter who sold herself to seafarers in order to obtain the three-hundred sacks of rice that her father, a blind man, had promised to a Buddhist monk. The offering of the rice and prayers to Buddha was to restore his sight. Unknown to her father, Shim Chong was taken by the seamen to the Indang Sea and sacrificed but later returned and became a queen. The poet here, however, has changed the father to a mother. Tr.

어머니가 나에게 가르쳐주신 말

인연은 재앙이니라—
내가 너무 배가 고파
어두움 속에
달덩이같이 삭발한 그리움을
하나 걸어두었더니
꿈인 듯 생시인 듯
이상한 향기 나는 白馬가 날아와
내가 하늘을 타고 갔느니라—
오색구름 속에 황금궤가 홀연히
걸려 있는데
너무 곱고 너무 신령하여
내가 그만 외상으로 너희들을
사오고 말았더니라—

인연은 재앙이니라—
뭉게뭉게 퍼져가는 암세포처럼
시시각각 외상값은 계속 불어나
강아지같이 불쌍한 내 새끼들아,
너희가 갚아야 하느니라,
맷돌을 목에 걸고 여기저기 쏘다니다
광견병 든 개처럼 맞아서 죽더라도
잔인한 것은 내가 아니다

Words My Mother Taught Me

Karma is misfortune!
Because I was so hungry,
I hung Longing, shorn like the moon,
in the dark.
Whether it was a dream or not,
a fragrant white horse flew over and
I got on it and flew into the sky.
Amid the colorful clouds was hung
a golden chest,
so pretty and mysterious,
that I just bought you, little ones,
on credit and brought you home.

Karma is misfortune!
Like cancer cells that bubble over and spread,
the debt grew every minute and second.
My poor little puppy-like babies!
You rush about, here and there,
with millstones around your necks.
Even were you to die like rabid dogs beaten to death,
it was not I who was cruel.
A blood-sucker I am not.

흡혈귀는—나는—아니다

고문처럼 질긴
철천지의 사랑—
이 무슨 원한의 달콤한
피 냄새—나는—
아니다—내 착한 새끼들아
사랑은 우환이니라—
인연은 후환이니라—

As tough as torture,
her love will cut through the universe:
What is this sweet smell of blood,
of my bitter resentment?! No, I am
not. My good little babies,
love is a worrisome malady;
karma is the evil consequence of it.

萬波息笛

—남편에게

더불어 살면서도
아닌 것같이,
외따로 살면서도
더불음같이,
그렇게 사는 것이 가능할까?……

간격을 지키면서
외롭지 않게,
외롭지 않으면서
방해받지 않고,
그렇게 사는 것이 아름답지 않은가?……

두 개의 대나무가 묶이어 있다
서로 간에 기댐이 없기에
이음과 이음 사이엔
투명한 빈자리가 생기지,
그 빈자리에서만
불멸의 금빛 음악이 태어난다

그 음악이 없다면
결혼이란 악천후,
영원한 원생동물들처럼

The Legendary Flute of Shilla Dynasty*

Is it possible
to live
together, yet as if not, or
to live
apart, yet as if together?

To keep some distance between us,
yet not be lonely,
and while not lonely,
neither be interfered with:
wouldn't it be beautiful to live like that?

When two bamboo stalks are bound together,
they do not lean on each other, and
so the spaces where they meet are open.
It is only from that open space
that the golden music of immortality can be born.

Without such music,
marriage is only bad weather—
like some protozoa
that strangle each other

서로 돌기를 뻗쳐
자기의 근심으로
서로 목을 조르는 것

더불어 살면서도
아닌 것같이
우리 사이엔 투명한 빈자리가 놓이고
풍금의 내부처럼 그 사이로는
바람이 흐르고
별들이 나부껴,

그대여, 저 신비로운 대나무 피리의
전설을 들은 적이 있는가?……
외따로 살면서도
더불음같이
죽순처럼 광명한 아이는 자라고
악보를 모르는 오선지 위로는
자비처럼 서러운 음악이 흘러라……

with their arms extended by worry.

Though we live
together yet as if not,
there is transparent space between us.
As in the interior of a pipe organ,
a breeze could flow and stars could flutter
through it.

My dear Spouse, have you ever heard of the legend
of the mysterious bamboo reed?
When they live apart,
yet as if together,
a radiant child will grow like a bamboo shoot,
and on the staff of some unknown musical score,
sorrowful music will flow like compassion.

---

* The "Man-pa-shik-chok" is a legendary flute, of the Shilla Period (B.C. 57-A.D. 935), which brought, if played, all human desires to fulfillment. Tr.

미완성을 위한 연가

Love Song for the Unfinished

미완성을 위한 연가

—경주 남산의 새기다만 마애불 앞에서

하나의 아름다움이 익어가기 위해서는
하나의 슬픔이
시작되어야 하리
하나의 슬픔이 시작되려는
저물무렵 단애 위에 서서
이제 우리는 연옥보다 더 아름다운 것을
꿈꾸어서는 안 된다고
서로에게 깊이 말하고 있었네

하나의 손과 손이
어둠 속을 헤매여
서로 만나지 못하고 스치기만 할 때
그 외로운 손목이 할 수 있는 일은
다만 무엇인지 알아?
하나의 밀알이 비로소 썩을 때
별들의 씨앗이
우주의 맥박 가득히 새처럼
깃을 쳐오르는 것을
그대는 알아?

하늘과 강물은 말 없이 수천년을 두고
그렇게 서로를 쳐다보고 있었네
쳐다보는 마음이 나무를 만들고

Love Song for the Unfinished

—Before an unfinished stone image of Maifreya on Mt. Nam San, Kyong-Ju

In order for beauty to ripen,
grief must begin.
Just as grief was beginning,
at dusk, we stood at the edge of a cliff:
"We must not dream
anything more beautiful now
than an inferno,"
we swore to one another.

Hand for hand
groping in the dark,
not meeting,
only grazing:
do you know
what one lonely hand can do?
Only when a grain of wheat dies
do the seeds of stars,
filling the pulse of the Universe,
lift up their wings like birds:
Do you understand?

Sky and river, without a word,
for thousands of years,

쳐다보는 마음이 별빛을 만들었네
우리는 몹씨 빨리 더욱 빨리
재가 되고 싶은 마음뿐이었기에
어디에선가, 분명,
멈추지 않으면 안 되었네,
수갑을 찬 손목들끼리
성좌에 묶인 사람들끼리

하나의 아름다움이 익어가기 위해서는
하나의 그리움이 시작되어야 하리,
하나의 긴 그리움이 시작되려는
깊은 밤 단애 위에 서서
우리는 이제 연옥보다 더 아름다운 것은
필요치가 않다고
각자 제 어둠을 향하여 조용히 헤어지고
있었네……

have stared at each other.
That staring heart made the trees;
that staring heart made the starlight.
We only had the heart
to turn, quickly, very quickly,
to ashes.
Somewhere, we definitely
had to stop:
handcuffed wrists to handcuffed wrists,
people bound to people
in a constellation.

For beauty to ripen,
longing must begin,
Deep in the night, as longing
was about to begin,
we stood at the edge of a cliff:
now, we say, we do not need
anything more beautiful
than an inferno,
and we each quietly part into
a darkness of
our own.

곡비(哭婢)

우는 것 이외에는
다른 아무것도 할 줄 몰라
나는 다만 우는 것으로
세상에 취업하였네,
바람이 지나갈 때도
작은 사랑이 두근두근 발밑으로
실핏줄을 풀며 지진처럼 흘러갈 때도
나는 다만 우는 것으로
그 아름다움에 참여하였네,

이솝은 노예였다네,
어쩌면 노예의 눈에만
더 많은 세상이 보이는 건지도 몰라,
슬픔의 인화지야말로 세상에서 가장
현상이 잘되는
인화지라는 것을
이솝을 만든 신이여, 전능하신
그대는 알려 주고 싶었던 건지도 몰라,

우는 것 이외에는
다른 아무것도 할 줄 몰라
나는 다만 우는 것으로

Wailer

Not knowing what to do
but cry,
I have been hired by the world
to cry.
Even when a breeze blew
and when tiny love flowed beneath my feet,
melting my small veins
with the jolt of an earthquake,
I only took part in their beauty
by crying.

Aesop was a slave.
Perhaps the world is more visible only through the eyes of a slave.
Photographic paper made of sorrow
is the most sensitive paper.
Perhaps that is what God, the Almighty, who made Aesop,
wanted us to know.

Not knowing what to do
but cry,
I have been hired by the world

세상에 취업하였네,
말하지 말라, 우는 사람이
비참한 사람이라고는,
말하지 말라, 제발,
나의 불행을
울음으로 축성하는 것이
부도덕한 광기라고는,

신은 태초에 달걀(卵)을 만드셨지,
알 속에 낙원이
낙원 속에 알이 있었으니
신은 미소하여 이곳을 떠나셨지,
그리고 달걀이 어느날 깨어지면서
우주의 지도가 생기니
그것이 창생의 상처였지,
어제도 오늘도 흐르는 피
오늘도 내일도 떨리는 상처

그 상처의 지도를 인화하기 위하여
나의 몇은 순결하고
나는 오직 울음으로써만
세상에 고용되었나니,

to cry.
Don' t ever tell me, please,
that it is immoral madness
to build a wall around my unhappiness by crying.

God made an egg in the beginning.
Paradise was in the egg
and the egg in paradise.
God left with a smile.
One day the egg broke
and a map of the universe was created.
That was the wound of creation:
the blood that flowed yesterday and flows today;
the wound that trembles today and will tomorrow.
In order to print that map of wounds
I wail simply,
as I am only hired by the world
to cry.
The hired wailer
walks at the head of the funeral cortege
and leaves the gravesite
last:

곡비는
장례의 가장 앞에 가고
무덤에서 가장 늦게 내려오는
실낙원의 도배사

the wallpaper hanger

of the lost paradise.

육십이 되면

육십이 되면
나는 떠나리라
정든 땅 정든 집을 그대로 두고
장롱과 식기와 냄비들을 그대로 두고
육십이 되면 나는
떠나리라
갠지스 강가로

딸아, 안녕히,
그동안 난 너를 예배처럼 섬겼으니,
남편이여, 그대도 안녕,
그동안 그렸던 희비의 쌍곡선을
모두 잊어주게,
축하한다는 것은 용서한다는 것,
그대의 축하를 받으며
난 이승의 가장 먼 뱃길에 오르리

생명의 일을 모두 마친 사람들이
갠지스 강가에 누워
태양의 괴멸작용을 기다린다는 곳,
환시인 듯

When I Turn Sixty

When I turn sixty
I will leave.
I will leave my beloved land, my beloved home,
my chests, dishes, pots and pans.
I will leave
when I turn sixty
for the Ganges.

Dear Daughter, farewell.
I have served you all this time as I would at a church service.
Dear Husband, you too, farewell.
Please forget all the waves we made between happiness
and unhappiness.
To congratulate is to forgive:
so I should receive your congratulations
as I set out on the longest voyage of this world

to that place where they who have finished all the business of
living
lie along the Ganges and
wait to decompose under the sun.
As in a fantasy,

허공 중에 만다라花가 꽃피며,
성스러운 재와 오줌이 혼합된
더러운 갠지스 물을 마시며
이승의 정죄와 저승의 빛을
구한다는
더러운 순결의 나라로

해골의 분말이 물 위에 둥둥 뜨면
해와 달과 별이
그려진 거대한
수레바퀴가 반짝반짝 혼령을 실어나르고
미쳐도
오직 신령으로 미친 사람들이
죽음의 천궁도를 들여다보며
환생을 근심하는 찬란한
강가

난 그 강가로 가리
힌 두의 장법대로
붉은 천 하나 몸에 두르고
어느 날 햇빛 아래 문득 쓰러지면
힌두의 승려들이 나를 태워주겠지

the flowers of the mandala bloom in the void, and
people seek the absolution of their sins in this world and the
light of the world to come
as they drink the dirty waters of the Ganges,
a mixture of sacred ashes and urine—
in the dirty land of the pure.

When the ashes of the skeletons float on the surface of the
water,
a huge wheel painted with sun, moon, and stars quickly
transports the spirits;
and even the crazed—
they are crazed only by the sacred spirits—
look at the map of the heavenly palace
and worry about reincarnation—
on this glorious river bank.

I am going to that river bank.
Following Hindu funeral practice,
I will drape a length of red cloth over myself
and collapse one day under the sun
and the Hindu monks will cremate me.

저승돈 삼십 냥을 빈손에 들고
나는 끝으로 말하리라
부디 사리를 채취하지 말아주게,
마치 모닥불 위에 장미꽃잎을 얹은
것처럼
그리고 그 불은 아름답겠지

해골의 분말이
그 강위에 뿌려지면
난 저승으로 가지 않고
이곳으로 오리,
한강이 되어 섬진강이 되어
광주 어귀의 극락강이 되어
어머니의 나라 딸의 나라
내 원죄의 나라로

육십이 되면
그러나 나는 떠나리라
성회(聖灰)와 식수가 뒤섞인
그 이상한 나라,
뼈 한 점 한 점마다
환각의 약초가 피어나고

Holding 30 coins in my bare hand,

I will speak for the last time.

Please do not collect my sarira.*

Like a rose petal upon a bonfire,

the fire would be beautiful.

When the ashes of my bones

are scattered upon the river,

I won't go to the other world

but will return home

as water of the Han River, the Seom-jin River, and

the River of Mandala at the entrance of Kwangju;

I will return to the land of my mother and of my daughter,

the land of my original sin.

But when I turn sixty,

I will leave nevertheless:

for that mysterious country

where sacred ashes and drinking water are mixed;

where from the smallest particles of bones, the hallucinatory
 medicinal herbs grow,

where sorrow is perfectly sterilized,

슬픔이 완전 소독되고
임종의 오줌 안에서
뱀이 불 같은 머리를 트는 그곳으로,
죽음마저 차마 예술이 되는
끝없는 끝의
그 먼 나라로

where snakes raise their heads like flames
during the final urination;
to that distant land
at the end of the endless,
where even death becomes art.

---

* Sanskrit: relics obtained after the ritual cremation of a religious person. Tr.

달걀 속의 生

Life Within an Egg

객석에 앉은 여자

그녀는 늘 어딘가가 아프다네.
이런데가 저런데가
늘 어느 곳인가가.

아프기 때문에
삶을 열렬히 살 수가 없노라고
그녀는 늘상 자신에게 중얼거리고 있지.

지연된 꿈, 지연된 사랑
유보된 인생
이 모든 것은 아프다는 이름으로 용서되고
그녀는 아픔의 최면술을
항상 자기에게 걸고 있네.

난 아파,
난 아프기 때문에
난 너무도 아파서

그러나 그녀는 아마도 병을 기르고
있는 것만 같애.

삶을 피하기 위해서

A Woman Sitting in the Audience

She says she is always hurting somewhere:
here or there,
always somewhere.

Because she is sick,
she cannot live her life with enthusiasm;
she is always mumbling to herself.

Dreams delayed, love delayed,
life retained:
these are all forgiven in the name of her aches
and with these she hypnotizes herself.

I am sick.
Because I am sick...
because I am too sick...

But it seems
she is cultivating her disease

in order to avoid life,
in order to forgive herself for avoiding life,

삶을 피하는 자신을 용서해 주기 위해서
살지 못했던 삶에 대한 하나의 변명을
마련하기 위해서
꿈의 상실에 대한 알리바이를 주장하기 위해서!

그녀는 늘 어딘가가 아프다네.
이런데가 저런데가
늘 그저 그런 어떤 곳이.

in order to prepare an excuse
for the life that she could not live,
in order to affirm an alibi for the loss of her dreams!

She says she is always hurting somewhere:
here or there,
always some ol' place....

일회용 시대

사발면을 후루룩 마시고
일회용 종이컵을 딱 구겨서 버리는 것처럼,
상처가 아물면
일회용 반창고를 딱 떼어서 던져넣는 것처럼

이 시대에
내가 누구를 버린다 해도
누구에게서 내가
버림받는다 해도

한번 입고 태워버리는 종이 옷처럼,
한번 사용하고 팽개쳐야 하는
콘돔처럼,
커피 자동판매기 안에서
눈을 감고 주루룩 쏟아져 내리는
희게 질린 종이컵처럼
껌종이처럼
일회용 설탕 포장지처럼

그렇게
내가 나를 버릴 수 있을까
그렇게

The Age of the Disposable

Just as we crumple and discard
a disposable cup after slurping our instant noodles;
just as we peel off a band aid and throw it away
when our cut heals—

In this day and age,
if I were to abandon someone,
or if I were
to be abandoned by someone:

like a paper dress you burn after one use;
like a condom
you toss after a single use;
like a terrified white paper cup
dropped blindly from a coffee vending machine;
like a gum wrapper or
the paper packet
for a spoonful of sugar—

Can I discard myself
just like that?
Can I, too, discard myself like that?

나도 나를 버릴 수 있을까

어느 으슥한 호텔 욕실에서
잠깐 쓰고 버려지는
슬픈 향내의
일회용 종이비누처럼…

like a disposable bar of soap

with sad scent,

used for a moment and discarded

in some dark hotel bathroom....

시인

이 일회용 도시 속에서
나는
제사에 쓰이는 꽃과도 같다.

우주에 내버려진
검은 융단 위에
밤마다
몸을 찔러
피의 자수를 놓고 있는 사람.

가난한 시인의 대명사
박정만이 타계한 후
KBS는 그의 삶을 놓고
얼마나 많은 드라마 시청률을 올렸는가.

이 일회용 도시속에서
우리는
매우 원시적인
불꽃祭物을 닮았다.

The Poet

In this disposable city
I am
like the flowers used for memorial services for our ancestors.

On the dark carpet thrown into the universe,
I am she who embroiders with blood,
Puncturing her body
every night.

After the death of Chung-Man Park,*
the synonym for poverty-stricken poets,
how much did KBS raise its ratings
by discussing his life?

In this disposable city
we very much resemble
the sacrifice offered by fire
in primitive times.

Park Chung Man (1946-1988): poet. Tr.

내가 없는 한국문학사

나는 무의미시 순수시의 시대에
순수시를 쓰지 않았고
참여시의 시대에도
참여시를 쓰지 않았다.(쓰지 못했다)
나는 80년대 한국시사의
알 라 모드
해체시의 시대에도
해체시를 쓰지 않았고 (못했고)
상업주의적 사랑시의 시대에
사랑시를 쓰지 못했으며 (않았으며)
민중시의 시대에도
민중시를 쓰지 않았다. (쓰지 못했다)

요즈음 말로 한다면
독재 지배 이데올로기를 방조해 온
매판미학의 일부
흉칙한……
(오, 맙소사, 난 내 죄가 그렇게
추한지 몰랐고
다른 죄도 많기 때문에
난 정말 상처와 피고름으로 인각된
거북이 등처럼 균열된—무늬—

The History of Korean Literature without Me

I did not write "pure" poems
in the age of meaningless, "pure" poetry.
I did not write (could not write) "engaged" poems
in the age of "engaged" poetry.
In the '80s, the a la mode period of
Korean poetry,
the period of deconstruction poetry,
I did not write deconstruction poems (I could not write them).
In the era of commercial love poetry
I could not write love poems (I did not write them).
In the age of Min-joong* poetry,
I did not write Min-joong poems (I could not write them).

In today's parlance
I am part of the sold-out esthetics
that stood by the dictatorial ideology;
the ugl...
(O God forbid! I never knew my crime
was so grotesque!
Because I have so many other sins,
I am like the back of a turtle,
a shattered pattern engraved with wounds and bloody pus—

혼비백산을 움켜잡고
언제나 임종전야—언어에
목을 매달고)
아뭏든, 언어가 나의 아멘이었었지.

어느 날 산사에서
하얀 벽지 위에 쥐벼룩이 기어가는
것을 보았다.
손톱으로 막 누르니까
일점 피를 남겼다.
우향좌, 좌향우 같은
어중간 나에게서도
그런 일점 피가 나올까.
깨끗이 도배된 벽지처럼 무늬맞춰 발라진
한국문학사 앞에서
나 오늘 한 마리 쥐벼룩
여류 쥐벼룩 (이곳에서 방점은 매우 중요하다)
구원은 없더라도
아멘을! 멈출 줄 모르는 아멘을!
멈출 수가 없으니……

grabbing hold of my own shattered soul
and always as if it were the night before my death—
betting my neck on language.)
Anyway, language was my Amen.

One day at a temple in the mountains,
I saw a tiny flea
crawling on some white wallpaper.
When I crushed it with my fingernail,
it left a spot of blood.
In the indeterminate middle—
my eyes right when turning left, my eyes left when turning right—
will there be a spot of my blood?
Before the History of Korean Literature
with its patterns matching like a neatly papered wall,
I am like a flea—
a female flea (here the bold is very important!).
Even if there is no redemption,
I cannot stop...
The Amens! The unstoppable Amens!

---

* Min-Joong is the term used during the 1980s to refer to the political, social, and artistic movements which had the "people" in mind. Tr.

제목 없는 사랑

죽어 버릴까.
아니면 이 불행한 삶을
계속해야 하나
해질 무렵이면
언제나 화두처럼 떠오르는 이 질문을
가슴에 안고
아가를 업은 나는 골목을 서성인다.

이혼을 할까,
아니면 이 우울한 결혼을
계속할 것인가,
가령 이 질문은 언제나 그 질문과 같아서
서울에서 가장 붐비는
롯데백화점 앞 네거리 스타트라인 위에서
갑자기 시동이 꺼져 버린 중고차처럼
사방에서 경음기소리가 들려오는데
혼자서 울고만 싶은 백치성이 있다.

절망 때문에 결혼을 하여
그 절망을 두 배로 만들고
허무 때문에 자식을 낳아
그 허무를 두 배로 만들었으니

Love for No Reason

Shall I kill myself,
or am I to continue in
this unhappy life?
Around sunset,
keeping in my heart this question that always arises
like a Zen riddle,
I linger in the alleyway with my baby
on my back.

Shall I divorce,
or am I to continue
in this gloomy marriage?
But this question is so much like the other
that I feel like a fool wanting to cry all by myself
in the midst of alarms ringing everywhere:
like an old car that suddenly dies
at the intersection in front of Lotte Department Store,
the busiest part in Seoul.

Because of despair, I married
and doubled the despair, and
because of emptiness, I had children

자꾸만 약효가 안 듣는 약을
자가처방하고 있는
너를 무엇이라고 불러야 하나.
해질 무렵이면
약방의 진열대 뒤에 서서
자꾸만 이름모를 약을 조제하고 있는
하얀 슬픔의 가운을 걸친
너를.
약효를 남먼저 시험해 보느라고
두 눈을 감고 자꾸만 쓰디쓴 약을
삼켜 보고 있는 너를.

아가를 업고
서성이는 골목길 안에서
나는 너 때문에 눈시울이 뜨거워진다.
네가 만든 영화 속에
나는 몹시 아픈 환자의 역할을 맡은
약물시음용 배우인 것만 같다.

and doubled the emptiness.

What should I call you,
who keep prescribing medicine
that does not work;
you who stand behind the counter
in a white coat of sadness
as dusk gathers,
and keep concocting medicines
with unknown names;
you who swallow the bitter medicine,
your eyes closed,
to test its effects
before anyone else?

In the alley where I linger
with my baby on my back,
my eyes swell with tears because of you.
In the film you are making,
I am like the actor with the role of
a seriously ill patient, the subject of
a medicinal experiment.

달걀 속의 生 · 1

우리는 꿈꾸지,
삶을 위하여
좀더 강해졌으면 하고,
보다 견고한 집을 짓고 싶고
더욱 안전한 껍질을 원하네,
마치 몰락이 없이
차갑게 버티고 있는
벽처럼
진짜로 강해질 수 있다면,
우리는 스스로 철교처럼
결코 폭파될 수 없는
어떤 희망을 구하지,
전혀 희망이 없이

그리고 또한 우린 알고 있어,
우주에 내버려진
하나의 달걀
과도 같이
그대와 나는
어둠 속에 둥둥 떠 있는
버림받은 허술한 알[卵]이라는 것을,
수문이 열리면

Life Within an Egg · 1

We dream, don't we,
that we can become only stronger:
for the sake of our life,
we want to build an even more solid house,
an even safer shell.
If only we could be as sturdy
as a wall that stands cold and
will never know collapse!
We seek certain hope,
like a steel bridge
that will never be demolished,
though there is no hope.

And we also know
that, like an egg
tossed into the universe,
you and I are loose eggs,
abandoned,
floating aimlessly in darkness.
When the flood gates open
and the flow of water tumbles out, unannounced,
a small water bubble is thrust into it:

제목도 없이 무너져 내리는
저녁물결 속에 고요히 으깨지는
조그만 수포
그리도 꿈 같은 고통

하얀 달걀이 하나
뜨거운 물 속에서 펄펄 끓고 있네,
찐달걀 속에선 어떤 부화의 깃도
돋아나질 않아,
무섭도록 고요한 침묵들의 비명,
(달걀꾸러미 속에 얌전히 누워 있는
하얀 찐계란들의 꽉찬 평화)
무섭게 달궈진 프라이 팬 위에서
성녀처럼 와들와들 해체되는
스크럼블드 에그,
어떤 꿈도 그 고통을 구할 순 없지

우주에 둥둥 떠 돌고 있는 독방
처럼
헐벗고, 외로운,
달걀 속에서
우린 한번 밖에 없는 자신의 삶을

pain so great, as though in a dream.

A small white egg
rapidly being boiled in hot water
(feathers will never hatch
from a boiled egg)
screams out of a silence that is terrifyingly calm
(the complete peace of boiled white eggs,
lying quietly nestled in straw).
A scrambled egg disintegrates
in a scorching-hot frying pan,
trembling like a woman saint:
in no dream will its pain
be relieved.

As though in a solitary room floating in the universe,
we spend our lives, which happen only once,
inside a barren and lonely egg.
We are sad because it lacks roots; and especially because it
lacks roots,
it is a white conclusion
after

꾸리고 있네,
뿌리가 없어 무엇보다도 뿌리가 없어 슬프지만
이름 없는 운동
뒤에
하얀 결말,

모든 달걀은 와삭와삭 깨어져
무참히 와해되고 말지만
그 안에 방이 있어
방이 하나 있어
내 얼굴을 닮은 조그만 양초 하나가
고요히 빛을 뿌리며 타오르고 있지,
눈물과 함께
입술연지로
환한 미소를 은은히 뿌리면서

a nameless exertion.

All the eggs will break
and be mercilessly shattered,
but it is a room,
a room
in which a small candle resembling my face
burns quietly, shedding light.
Spreading quietly, my bright smile
with lipstick
has been touched by tears.

달걀 속의 生 · 2

냉장고 문을 열면 달걀 한 줄이
온순히 꽂혀 있지,
차고 희고 순결한 것들
아무리 배가 고파도
난 그것들을 쉽게 먹을 순 없을 것 같애

교외선을 타고 갈곳없이 방황하던 무렵,
어느 시골 국민학교 앞에서
초라한 행상 아줌마가 팔고 있던
수십 마리의 그 노란 병아리들,
미분지곽 속에서 바글바글 끓다가
미분지곽 위로 보글보글 기어오르던
그런 노란 것들이
(생명의 중심은 그렇게 따스한 것)
살아서 즐겁다고 꼬물거리던 모습이
살아서 불행하다고 늘상 암송하고 있던
나의 눈에 문득 눈물처럼 다가와 고이고

그렇다면 나는 여태 부화를 기다리고 있던
중이었을까,
아아, 얼마나 슬픈가,
차가운 냉장칸 맨 윗줄에서

Life Within an Egg · 2

When I open the refrigerator door, there is a row of eggs,
obediently arrayed;
cold, white, pure:
no matter how hungry I might be,
I cannot eat them so easily.

While I was out and about, having taken a suburban line,
but with nowhere to go,
a poor woman was selling
yellow chicks by the ten
in front of a rural elementary school.
The chicks were seething inside a card–board box
and then bubbled over the run,
those yellow things
(life at the center is so warm).
The image of those chicks seething, happy just to be alive,
caught in my eyes and suddenly welled up like tears,
in me, who have been reciting just how unhappy I am to be
alive.

Does this mean that I have been waiting all this time to hatch?
How sad!

달걀껍질 속의 흰자위와 노른자위는
무슨 꿈들을 꾸고 있을까,
중풍으로 쓰러진 아버지의 병실에서
입원비 걱정을 하고 있는 우리 가난한 형제들처럼
흰자위와 노른자위도
무슨 그런 절망의 의논들을 하고 있을 것인가

사계절 전천후 냉장고
하얀 문을 조용히 열면
추운 달걀들의 속삭임 소리가 들리는 것 같다,
엄마 엄마 안아줘요 따스한 품속에
어미 닭에 안기지 못하고 만 달걀들처럼
희망 소비자 가격보다 더 싸게 팔려온
너희들처럼
나도 역시 여권이 분실된 사람
희망의 온도가 차츰 내려갈 때
오히려 절망은 조용하고 초연해지는 것 같지,

On the top shelf of a cold refrigerator,
what dreams can an egg yolk and white
possibly have inside their shell?
In the hospital room where my father is lying, stricken by a stroke,
my brothers and sisters worry about the hospital expenses.
Are the egg yolk and white
carrying on a discussion in a despair like ours?

The refrigerator for all seasons: in any season,
if I quietly open the white door,
I can almost hear whispering among the frigid eggs.
Mommy, Mommy, please hold me in your arms and keep me warm!
Like eggs that have never been held by their mother hen,
Like those sold cheaper than the suggested retail price,
I, too, am a person without a passport.
As the temperature of hope gradually falls,
my despair seems to become ever more tranquil and detached.

하나를 위하여

나는 많은 것을 원하지 않는다.
단지 하나가 되고 싶을 뿐이다.
살았던 것들 중
그 중 아름다운 하나가,
슬펐던 것들 중
그 중 화사한 하나가,
괴로웠던 것들 중
그 중 순결한 하나가 되고 싶을 뿐이다.

나는 많은 길을 원하지 않는다.
오히려 더 많은 길을 버리고 싶고
더 많은 꿈을 지우고 싶고
다만 하나의 길과
다만 하나의 꿈을 통하여
물방울이 물이 되고
불꽃들이 불이 되는
그 하나의 비밀을 알고 싶을 뿐이다.

하나를 이루기 위하여
그 하나에 닿기 위하여
나는, 하나 하나, 소등 연습을 해야 할는지도
모른다.

For the Sake of Being One

I don't want many things.
I just wish to be "one";
of all the things that have lived,
I want to be one of the beautiful;
of all the things that are saddened,
I want to be one of the glorious;
of all the things that have suffered,
I want to be one of the innocent.

I do not want many roads.
I would rather be rid of them;
I would rather erase my many dreams.
Only by one road
and with one dream
do I wish to learn the secret of
drop-upon-drop becoming water
and spark-after-spark becoming fire.

To become one,
to arrive at one,
I may have to try putting out all the lights,
one by one.

가로등이 다 꺼진 어둠 속으로
솜처럼 착하게 다 적셔져서
세상에서 가장 아름답게 타오르는
하나의 봉화가 되고 싶은지도 모른다.

In the darkness, where no street lamps are lit,
saturated like a soft piece of cotton,
I might want to become a bonfire and
burn ever so beautifully in the world!

평화일기 · 1

인생이란 그런 것일까.
저녁을 먹고, 조립식 의자에 엉성하게 앉아
양파껍질을 벗기고 있을 때
미운 일곱 살 말 안 듣는 딸아이가
TV 채널을 이리저리 돌리고 있다.

찰칵찰칵 화면은 신속히 돌아가면서
한쪽에선 청순가련형 미모의 여배우가
알지 못할 대사를 읊조리면서
우산 아래서 울고 있는데
다른 한쪽에선 수사반장
살인추리극을 하고
또다른 채널에선 젊음의 록 콘서트
우주인 복장의 젊은 남녀 가수가
오 팔레스타인 팔레스타인 하면서
시야 가득히 환상적인 광물로 가득찬
우주의 무대를 둥둥 펼치고 있다.

오, 모가지가 없는 나의 몸뚱이
오, 몸뚱이가 없는 나의 모가지.
위로.
저벅저벅 날은 저물고

Peace Diary · 1

Is life like that?
After dinner, as I sit sloppily on a folding chair
peeling onions,
my seven-year-old daughter is stubbornly
flipping here and there through the channels.

Click, click: the screen changes rapidly.
In one scene an actress of delicate and innocent beauty,
mouthing something unintelligible,
is crying under an umbrella;
in another, a detective is investigating a
murder mystery;
in yet another, two rock singers, a young man and woman
dressed in astronaut's suits,
are singing "O, Palestine, Palestine"
and fill my vision with the stage
of the universe,
filled with fantastic minerals.

O, my body without a head!
O, my head without a body!
Consolation:

아무도 나를 구원하러 오지 않는 것처럼
나도 누구를 구원하러 떠나지 않으며
이리저리 돌아다니는 화면을 바라보면서
양파껍질을 벗기는
손을 부지런히 움직이다가
누가 범인이고 누가 착한 사람인지조차
알 수가 없어서
다시 수사반장을 보려고 하는데
그 채널에선 이제 막 아방궁 같은
욕조에서 빠져나온 알몸의 여인이
아름다운 머리를 감는
향긋한 샴푸선전이 흘러나오고 있다.

인생이란 정말 그런 것일까.
양파껍질을 부지런히 벗기다가
문득 손을 멈추고
가만히 양파를 더듬어 찾았을 때
양파는 아주 없어져 버리고
양파껍질만 희미한 회억의 넝마처럼
무릎 위에 수북히 쌓여있는 것.
이 엉성한 조립이 나의 삶을 이끌어 가고
그렇듯이 TV 밖으로 세상 밖으로

the day is growing ominously dark.
Just as no one comes to rescue me,
neither do I go to rescue anyone.
Glancing at the screen jumping from one to another,
I busy my hands peeling onions.
I cannot figure out who the bad guy is
or who the good guy.
So I try watching the detective again.
Just then, a naked woman steps out of
a luxurious bathtub and begins to wash her beautiful hair
in a fragrant commercial for shampoo.

Is life really like that?
In the midst of busily peeling an onion,
I suddenly stop to look
for the onion,
but the onion has disappeared for good:
only the skins are piled up on my lap,
like shreds of faint memories.
This haphazard assembly governs my life
and thus, while floating and flowing
beyond the TV, beyond this world,

괄호 밖으로, 둥실둥실 떠내려 가면서,
모가지가 없는 나의 몸뚱이와
몸뚱이가 없는 나의 모가지가
잠시 기구한 인연처럼 스치기도 하는
이 사악한 평화.

beyond the parentheses,
my body without a head
and my head without a body
meet each other as if by some unlucky karma:
a vicious peace!

평화일기 · 2

가출을 할까
출가를 할까
이것은 나의 영원한 테마이다.
누군가도 그러하리라.
가출을 하든지
출가를 하든지
어딘가에 평화를 구하러 가고 싶은 심정으로
밤은 저문다.

신촌로터리에서 지하철 구멍 속으로 들어가면
삼분 자동칼라 사진실이 있지.
시든 베이지색 커튼을 밀치고
들어가면
관 속같이 하얀 네모난 방.
나는 주섬주섬 주머니 속의 동전들을
모조리 꺼내놓고
일금 이천오백원이 될 때까지
동전들을 고백처럼 밀어넣으며
플래시가 번쩍 하는 동안의
그 작은 재회를 사고 싶다.

동전이 찰칵찰칵 들어가 액수가 차면

Peace Diary · 2

Should I run away from home?
Should I leave it for good?*
This is an eternal question for me.
Others must ask themselves the same question,
whether to run away from home,
or to leave it for good.
With night comes the desire
to find peace somewhere.

If you go down into the hole that leads to the subway
at Shin-chon Circle,
there is a three-minute, serve-yourself color-photo studio.
If you go in, pushing aside the tired beige curtain,
there is a square, white room like the inside of a coffin.
I take out every coin in my pocket
until I have two-thousand five-hundred won
and slip them in as if they are confessions
and buy the tiny encounter, that lasts a flash-
pop.

The coins click in until the designated amount is reached,
and the light in the coffin goes off automatically.

관 속의 실내등은 저절로 꺼지고
어둠 속에 갇힌 채로
웃을까 말까 망설이는 동안
나의 인생은 그 일초동안의
찬란한 자동 마그네슘 불꽃 안에
영원한 우주의 중심으로 환생하게 된다.

따끈따끈 인화되어 나오는
나의 사진을 기다리며
나는 지하철 정류장을 오고가는 수많은
사람들을
바라본다.
모두다 어딘가로 떠나고 있고
모두다 어딘가로 닿고 싶은 사람들.

자동칼라 사진실의 출납창구 아래로
내 사진이 덜컥하고 완성되어 떨어질 때
나는 행복하다.
어제보다 더 늙었다든지
점점 더 괴상한 추녀가 되어간다고 해도
(추함만큼 우리에게 일상적인 게 또 있으랴)
나는 정말 관심이 없다.

Trapped in the dark,
I hesitate as to whether to smile or not.
My life returns to the center of the eternal universe
in that glorious burst of magnesium, for
one second.
Awaiting the hot prints of the picture,
I watch the innumerable people
coming and going through the subway station.
All are leaving for someplace
and all desire to arrive someplace.

When my photos drop with a clink
through the little opening,
I am happy.
That I am older than yesterday
or becoming more and more an ugly eccentric,
(what could be more ordinary than ugliness?)
I don' t really care.
The only thing I recall is the eternity
of that brief moment when I met myself, Mother, Womb.
The warm darkness is like home.
No one can tell me now

다만 나는 나와 만나는
그 짧은 순간의 영원. 어머니. 자궁.
고향 같은 따스한 어둠을 기억할 뿐.
아무도 이제 내가 안보인다고
말하지는 못하겠지.

나처럼
자기 스스로와 면회하고 싶은 객지의 사람들이
먼길을 걸어와
관같은 자동사진실 근처를
어슬렁거리고 있다.
호적이 없는 부랑자들처럼
니코틴에 물든 입술이 파랗다.

that I am invisible.

People from out-of-town who want to have a visit with them-
selves,
as I did,
walk a long way to come
and loiter around the coffin-like,
serve-yourself photo studio.
Like drifters with no permanent address,
they have lips blue from nicotine.

---

* The word "Ka-chool" means "to run away from home" and the word "Chool-ka," which is the reverse of "Ka-chool," means "to leave home permanently to enter a Buddhist monastery." They are composed of the same characters but reversed. Kim Seung-Hee uses many such words to make a play on words. Tr.

중심에 계신 어머니

내 몸의 한 가운데
居하고 계시는 것
배꼽 속에
멈추어
가만히 맴도는 것

멈추어 서있는 것
살아서 맴도는 것

횡액의 노른자위
그
생명의 꼭지가
아직 남아
언젠가 한몸이었던
분리
그 분리의 표적으로

그리고 혹은
혹은
나는 죽어도 사라지지 않는다는
19세기식 울부짖음처럼

Mother, at My Center

Living
within my body,
quietly circling,
caught at my belly button,
she has paused, and yet
is alive and circling.

Yolk of misfortune,
the cap of life
still remains,
a sign of separation—
a separation of what once was
one body.

And perhaps, like the scream of
the 19th century, it will not disappear,
even if I should die.

실비아 플라스

너는 어디에선가
오늘 새벽에도 또 죽고 있겠지,
고운 머리칼의 딸들과
아직 우유병을 빨고 있는
네 귀여운 아들을 이층 침대방에 잠재우고
살금살금 아래층으로 내려와
도둑고양이처럼
지하철 계단을 밟고

원, 세상에, 간밤에 이층여자가 죽었다는군,
식탁 위엔 제 새끼들을 위한 우유와
아침식탁을 준비해 놓고
보일러실의 가스를 틀고
잠옷바람으로 개처럼 뻗어 있드래, 글쎄,
끔찍하지, 암, 끔찍하고말고,
침과 오물과 토사물을 모조리 꺼내놓고
원, 세상에, 더럽기도 하지,
교수부인이라는 여자가

잠에서 깨어날 때마다
난 언제나 그렇게 내 시체가 앰블런스에 실려
이미 떠난 후였던 것 같다,

Sylvia Plath*

You must be dying again
somewhere, as dawn now is breaking.
Having tucked in your daughters with their pretty hair
and your adorable son still sucking on his bottle
in their upstairs bedrooms,
you quietly come downstairs
and go down the stairs to the basement
like an alley cat.

For heaven's sake! The woman upstairs died last night!
She set out milk and got breakfast ready
for her kids,
and turned on the gas in the furnace room.
She was found sprawled out like dog, in her night clothes, I heard.
Terrible! Just terrible!
Drool, filth, vomit all over the place!
How in the world...?! What a mess!
And a wife of a professor at that!

Whenever I wake from sleep,
it seems that my corpse has already left
like that, in an ambulance.

부시시한 머리로 부시시한 아침을 먹고 있는
나를 보면
사람의 일생이란 잘해봐야
자살골을 슛 골인 시키는 일 외에
무엇이 있을까,
오전과 오후가 광명의 보자기처럼
활짝 펼쳐지는 눈부신 대낮에 생각해보면
죽는다는 것이 꼭 포르노그라피 같고
한밤중에 문득 일이나 생각해보면
산다는 것이 또
포르노그라피 같은데

실비아 플라스,
넌 왜 아주 가지 않고
밤마다 내 침실 창 너머에
달빛 같은 검은 상복을 걸치고
안녕을 묻고 있지,
양쪽에 두 아이를 거느리고 누워 생각해보면
실비아 플라스,
자살과 상사병 사이엔 유사성이 있다고 하던
그 말이 에이즈 균처럼 떠오를 뿐이야

When I see myself having a thrown-together breakfast,
my hair all unkempt, I wonder
what else in life is there to do except, at best,
to shoot and make a goal, a suicide goal?
If I think about it during a sparkling midday
when morning and afternoon are spread out
like a kerchief of brilliant light,
dying seems pornographic.
And if I think of it, awake suddenly
in the middle of the night,
living also seems pornographic.

Sylvia Plath,
Why do you not just go away for good?
Why do you keep asking me how I am,
every night outside my bedroom window,
wearing black mourning clothes
like moonlight?
Lying with my two children at my sides, I think about
Sylvia Plath.
Someone once said suicide and lovesickness have similarities:
only these works keep coming to mind, like an Aids virus.

---

*American poet (1932~1963).

나혜석 콤플렉스

친구여, 나에겐 그런 두려움이 있다네,
저녁을 잘 먹고
실내악이 흐르는 유리창 앞에 고양이처럼 앉아
어둠이 글썽글썽
창문을 두드리는 시간이 오면
어디선가 아직 잠들지 못한 바람이 있어
풍선처럼 고요히
내 몸을 내가 찌르는
하얀 바늘의 살륙의 느낌 같은 것,
풍선 속의 바람은
고요히 스르르
마치, 아무 일도 아니라는 듯,
간단히 숨을 거두고
부네탈과 미얄탈 같은 것들이
벽 위에서 휴지처럼
구겨져 떨어지는 가벼운 시간

친구여, 세상엔 그런 여인들이 있었다고 하지,
가면을 벗어 조용히 응접실 탁자 위
가족사진 앞에 포개어 놓고
나의 시간도 아니고
너의 시간도 아닌

Na Hey-Seok Complex*

Dear friend, I have a certain fear.
After a pleasant dinner,
I sit, pretty as a cat on a window sill;
chamber music is flowing;
swelling darkness knocks at the window,
a wind from somewhere, not died down.
Quietly, as though it were a balloon,
I puncture my own body,
and feel death by a white needle.
The air in the balloon
silently leaks out,
as though nothing were amiss.
Simply, its breath ceases
and the mask of the housewife
and that of the granny
crumple and fall like tissues from the wall.
The hour of lightness.

Dear Friend, there were such women.
They took off their masks and set them on a shelf in the living
room,
next to the family portrait;

「가정의 날」이라는 영원한 반공일(半空日) 같은
어정쩡한 주부의 직업을 닫고
에미는 선각자였느니라—
추운 겨울날
다리를 건너간 여인들이 있었다고 하지

여인에겐 원래 횡단공포증 같은 것이 있어서
다리를 건널 땐 어지럽고 무서워
아버지나 남편의 팔장을 끼고 걷는 것인데
추운 겨울날,
홀로 다리를 건너간 여인들이 있었지,
부네와 미얄탈이 걸려진
실내악의 방을 나와
다리를 건너
피안으로 홀로 가는 여인들은 보여주지,
사자와 고양이는 똑같이 고양이과에 속한
맹금류의 동족인 것을,
여인들은 머리칼 위에 빛나는 야성의
화관을 쓰고
조용히 슬픈 선각의 사자후를 남겼네,
에미는 선각자였느니라—고

closed the door on their nondescript housewiving,
on "Family Day," the half-holiday,
which has nothing to do with you or me.
"Your mother was ahead of her time."
On a cold wintry day,
they crossed the bridge.

Women are supposed to be afraid of crossing the street.
They are supposed to feel dizzy and terrified crossing a bridge.
They walk arm-in-arm with their fathers or husbands.
But there were women who crossed bridges alone,
on cold wintry days.
They left the room filled with chamber music,
where the masks of housewife and old grandma hung,
and crossed the bridge;
alone on the other side they would tell us:
lion and cat are both feline,
the same species of ferocious animal.
Women wore flower garlands
shining wildly in their hair
and quietly left behind the doleful enlightenment of the lion's
mane.

그리고 나혜석은 거리에서 죽었어,
행려병자가 되어 쓰러지면서
그녀는 원시림 같은, 처녀림 같은,
산소용접으로 튀는 파란 불꽃 같은
쓰러지는 두 눈은 어둠 속에서 정녕
아름다웠지,
여자는 삼계(三界)에 집이 없어
아버지의 집도
남편의 집도
아들의 집도
여자의 집은 아니어서

친구여, 나에겐 그런 예감이 있다네,
나혜석은 죽어서도 옳게 묻히지 못하여
구천을 떠돌다가
이제 나에게로 와서
내 가슴을 위패삼아 머물고 있으니
나 또한 미신처럼
그녀의 신위(神位)를 비밀히 모시고 있으니
여자는
왜
자신의 집을 짓기 위하여

saying,
"Your mother was ahead of her time."

Na Hey-Seok died on the street.
She collapsed from her roaming.
She was like a primeval, virgin forest.
Like blue sparks flying from the tip of a welder' s torch,
her eyes as she fell in the dark were indeed
beautiful.
Women do not have a house in The Three Worlds:**
a father' s house,
a husband' s house,
a son' s house. Yes,
but not a woman' s house.

Dear friend, something tells me
that Na Hey-Seok was not buried properly. Even after her death
she roams about in Ninth Heaven.***
She comes to me now
and remains in me, my heart her spirit tablet.
I also, following the superstition,
secretly keep her spirit.

자신을 천지사방 찢어버리지 않으면 안 되는가,
검정나비처럼 흰나비처럼
여자는 왜
자신의 집을 짓기 위하여선
항상 비명횡사를 생각해야 하는가

Why
must a woman
tear herself to pieces
to build her own house?
Like a black butterfly, like a white butterfly,
why must a woman
who builds her own house
always face a miserable death?

---

* Na Hey-Seok (1896~1949) was the first Korean woman artist to work in the western-style of oil painting. She was educated in Japan and Europe. She was also a gifted writer and a few of her short stories remain.

** Trayo-dhatavah (Sanskrit)

*** The highest sky. In Buddhism, the nine heavens surrounding the earth. Tr.

성녀와 마녀사이

엄마, 엄마,
그대는 성모가 되어 주세요,
한국전래동화 속의 착한 엄마들처럼
참, 아니, 사임당 신씨
신사임당 엄마처럼 완벽한 여인이 되어
나에게 한평생 변함없는 모성의 모유를
주셔야 해요,
이 험한 세상
엄마마저, 엄마마저…… 난 어떻게……

여보, 여보,
당신은 성녀가 되어 주오,
간호부처럼 약을 주고 매춘부처럼
꽃을 주고 튼튼실실한 가정부도 되어
나에게 변함없이 행복한 안방을
보여주어야 하오,
이 험한 세상
당신마저, 당신마저……난 어떻게……

여자는 액자가 되어간다,
액자 속의 정물화처럼
고요하고 평화롭게,

Between Saint and Witch

Mommy, Mommy!
Please be holy,
like the good mothers of traditional Korean folk tales!
Well, no! More like Lady Shin Sa-Im-Dang.*
Be a perfect mother like Lady Shin Sa-Im-Dang
and give me
the milk of your maternal love,
unchanging and unceasing throughout your life.
In this tough world,
How can I...? If Mommy were to... If Mommy were to...

Honey, Honey!
Please be a saint!
Give me medicine as a nurse would, and like a prostitute
bring me flowers. Be a strong and solid homemaker,
and offer me
a living room where happiness lasts forever.
In this tough world,
How can I...? If you, dear, were to... If you, dear, were to···

Women are becoming framed pictures.
Like framed still life,

액자 속의 가훈(家訓)처럼
평화롭고 의젓하게,
여자는 조용히 넋을 팔아 넘기고
남자들의 꿈으로 미화되어
도배되어
「가화만사성」(家和萬事成) 액자 하나로
조용히 표구되어
안방의 벽에 애매하게 매달려 있다

모나리자의 미소는 웃는 것인가
우는 것인가,
그녀의 미소는 용서인가
배신인가,
난 알 수 없지만
난 그녀의 그림자 망사옷 같은
검은 가슴 속에서
무서운 화산의 힘을 두근두근 느낄 수 있지,
남자들의 꿈으로 미화될 수 없는
박제될 수 없는
마녀의 부엌 같은 뜨거운 화산이
그녀의 미소를
영원한 무서움으로 낯설게 만들고 있는데,

they are silent and peaceful;
like framed family mottos,
they are peaceful and dignified.
Women are quietly selling off their souls.
Made beautiful to make men dream,
pasted over a wallpaper mat,
turned quietly into a framed "Familial harmony accomplishes
all things,"
women hang unnoticed on the wall of the back room.

Could Mona Lisa's smile really be a laugh?
Or perhaps crying?
Is her smile forgiving?
Or does it show betrayal?
I have no way of knowing,
but I can feel the pounding force of a terrifying volcano
under her dark breast,
beneath her mesh clothing, like a shadow.
The volcano — hot as the kitchen of a witch,
that male fantasies cannot make beautiful
or stuff—
makes her smile

그녀는 애매하다,
성녀와 마녀 사이
엄마만으로도
아내만으로도
표구될 수 없는, 정복될 수 없는,
저 영원한 회오리의 명화는,
여인에게 사랑은 벌같은 것이지만
그러나 여인은 사랑을 통해
여신이 되도록 벌받고 있는 거라고
그녀는 스스로 영원을 표구하면서
세상을 배경으로 거느리고
늠름하게 서 있지

in a strange, eternal terror.

She is undefinable,
neither holy woman nor witch.
The great painting of an eternal tornado
can neither be framed nor conquered
as only a mother,
as only a wife.
Love is punishment to a woman.
But a woman is punished
to become a goddess through love.
She frames eternity herself,
commanding the world as her backdrop,
and stands tall.

---

* Lady Shin Sa-Im-Dang (1504～1551) is one of the most celebrated women of the Choson Dynasty (1392～1910). She was the mother of Prime Minister Yi Yool-Gok and was known for her wisdom as mother and wife, for her art work, and for her poetry. Tr.

엄마의 발

딸아, 보아라,
엄마의 발은 크지,
대지의 입구처럼
지붕 아래 대들보처럼
엄마의 발은 크지,

엄마의 발은 크지만
사랑의 노동처럼 크고 넓지만
딸아, 보았니,
엄마의 발은 안쪽으로 안쪽으로
근육이 밀려
꼽추의 혹처럼
문둥이의 콧잔등처럼
밉게 비틀려 뭉그러진 전족의
기형의 발

신발 속에선 다섯 발가락
아니 열 개의 발가락들이
도화선처럼 불꽃을 튕기며
아파아파 울고
부엉부엉 후진국처럼 짓밟히어
평생을 몸살로 시름시름 앓고

Mom's Feet

Look, dear Daughter,
Mom's feet are large, aren't they?
Like an entrance to the good earth,
like a beam under the roof,
Mom's feet are large.

Mom's feet are large,
large and wide like a labor of love.
But, dear Daughter, have you noticed?
Mom's feet are pushed more and more inward.
The muscles are all pushed inward
like the hump of a hunchback,
like the nose of a leper, or
the twisted and
deformed shape of bound feet.

Five toes inside the shoes,
or rather ten,
sending out sparks like the fuse of a bomb,
crying from the pain of
being stepped on at random, like underdeveloped nations
ailing from the flu all their lives.

엄마의 신발 속엔
우주에서 길을 잃은
하얀 야생별들의 무덤과
야생조들의 신비한 날개들이
감옥창살처럼 종신수로 갇히어
창백하게 메마른 쇠스랑꽃 몇 포기를
조화(弔花)처럼
우두커니 걸어놓고 있으니

딸아, 보아라,
가고 싶었던 길들과
가보지 못했던 길들과
잊을 수 없는 길들이
오늘밤 꿈에도 분명 살아 있어
인두로 다리미로 오늘밤에도 정녕
떠도는 길들을 꿈속에서 꾹꾹 다림질해 주어야 하느니
네 키가 점점 커지면서
그림자도 점점 커지는 것처럼
그것은 점점 커지는 슬픔의 입구,

세상의 딸들은
하늘을 박차는

Inside a mom's shoes
are tombs of the white unknown stars
that have been lost in the Universe,
mysterious wings of wild birds which
have been locked up for life behind prison bars,
a few bunches of pale flowers dried up and,
like artificial flowers,
hung up and forgotten.

Daughter, look.
The roads that I wanted to travel,
the roads that I have never traveled,
and the roads that I cannot forget,
still live on in my dreams tonight.
I must press hard the roads that I wander in my dreams,
using irons large and small.

As you grow taller,
your shadow also grows taller.
The entrance to sorrow grows large.

The daughters of the world have wings

날개는 가졌으나
세상의 여자들은 아무도 날지 못하는구나,
세상의 어머니는 모두 착하신데
세상의 여자들은 아무도
행복하지 않구나……

to beat the air with,

but no woman ever flies through the sky.

All the mothers of the world are good,

yet no woman in the world

is happy....

어떻게 밖으로 나갈까
How Can I Get Out

유목을 위하여 · 1

—누군가 토끼를 몰고 있다

누군가 토끼를 몰고 있다,
나는 신문을 던져 버린다,
누군가 토끼를 몰고 있다,
나는 TV를 꺼버린다,
신문도 안보고 TV도 꺼버린다면
나에겐 정말 할일이 없어진 기분이다,
아이들에게 공부나 좀 하라고
잔소리나 퍼붓는 일밖에는,
(나도 토끼를 몰고 있다. 나같은 토끼에게 또 몰릴 토끼가 있다는 게 먹이사슬의 이해할 수 없는 변주 같지만)

어느 사이엔가
우리는
누군지 모를 토끼를 몰고 있는
몰이꾼이거나
누군지 모를 토끼에게 몰리고 있는
몰리는 토끼이거나 하는 것이다,
(十三人의兒孩는무서운兒孩와무서워하는兒孩와그렇게뿐이 모였소. 〈다른事情은없는것이차라리나았소〉)처럼
지평의 속도 위에서는
단지 몰리는 불안과 모든 갈증이
있을 뿐,

For Nomads · 1

— Someone Is Chasing Rabbits

Someone is chasing rabbits:
I toss away the newspaper.
Someone is chasing rabbits:
I turn off the TV.
If I don't look at the newspaper and turn off the TV,
there seems to be nothing for me to do—
nothing except nag my kids
to study some.
(I also am chasing rabbits. It is such an incomprehensible variation
on the theme of the food chain that there are rabbits to be chased by a rabbit like me.)

Somehow we become
predators
who chase rabbits whom we don't know,
or the prey
chased by an unknown predator.
(Thethirteenchildrenconsistedoftheterrorrizingchildrenandthe terrifiedchildrengatheredthere.〈Thingswerebetteroffwithou t alltheotherthings〉)
With such earthly rapidity,

그리하여 멈출 수 없는
파시스트적 질주만이 있을 뿐

누군가 오늘도 토끼를 몰고 있다,
몰리는 토끼는 모는 토끼가 되고
모는 토끼는 또 몰리는 토끼가 되는
알 수 없는 공포의 수동태적 빙빙거림 속에서
밖으로 나가려는 토끼는
어디로 빠져나가야 하나?
몰리는 토끼로 살고싶지 않은 그만치
모는 토끼로도 살고싶지 않은
그는
어디로부터 욕망의 회로를 끊어
이 무서운 지평의 마수를 빠져나가는 구멍을
발견할(만들어낼) 것인가?

신문 속의 진저리나는 특호활자가
TV속의 위장된 뉴스특보가
백화점의 바겐세일 광고가
세금고지서 미납자동차세 독촉증서가
점점 떨어지는 아이의 성적표가
더욱더 대담해지는 여성지의 욕망들이

only the anxiety of prey and its pursuit exist,
and so does the unstoppable
fascist running.

Someone is chasing rabbits:
the rabbits preyed upon become the predators
the predators become the prey.
In the passive cycle of terror of the unknown,
where should a rabbit escape if it wants
to get away?
It does not want to live as a rabbit pursued
any more than it wants to live as a predator.
Where should it break the cycle of desire
and crawl through a hole to escape from the evil hands
in this terrifying land?

The sickening, gigantic headlines of the newspapers;
the special news reports on TV that are disguised;
advertisements for department-store bargain sales;
notices of overdue taxes and car registrations;
my children's declining grades;
women's magazines that, ever more daring, stir our desires;

우리로 하여금 그것에 복종하게 하고,
우리들을 지배하고 착취하는
그것을
더욱더 욕구하게끔 몰고 있지 않은가?

불쌍한 토끼는
지붕 위에 올라가 울고 있다,
울면서 피우는 하얀 담배연기는
화장터의 무슨 손수건 같기도 하고
도주를 도와달라고
먼 곳으로 보내는
하나의 봉화의 애소 같기도 하다.

Aren' t they bringing us to obey in everything
and pressing us to desire more and more the very things
that rule and exploit us?

The pathetic rabbit whimpers
on the roof top.
The white smoke rising from the cigarette
she is smoking as she weeps
resembles a handkerchief at the crematory,
or the sad plea of a bonfire
signaling to some far-off place
for help in escaping.

유목을 위하여 · 4
—괄호 안의 삶

외줄의 끈 위에 올라 있는
곡예사와도 같이
너는 산다,
아침일찍 나갔다 저녁늦게 돌아오는
지평 위의 너의 보행이라 해도
공중곡예의 외줄과도 같은
땅 이외의
다른 어떤 땅을 밟아본 적이 없다,
(선을 넘기는 그렇게 어려우니)

아침일찍 나가서
선 위의 상자곽 속으로 들어갔다
저녁늦게 나와서
선 위의 또다른 상자곽 속으로 들어가는
사람들, (고객감시 카메라 자동작동중)
아직까지 금 밖으로 나가본 적은
없다, (실탄휴대청경 비상근무중)
어떤 금일지라도
금을 위반한다는 것은 배제되고 밀려나고
추방되고 벗어나는 것이니
(선 위에서 네 발로 기어다니기)

For Nomads · 4

—Life in parentheses

You live
like an acrobat
poised upon a tight rope.
Even if you walk on the surface of the earth,
leaving home early in the morning and returning late in the
  evening,
you never step upon any ground
but the tight rope of the acrobat.
(To step off the rope is so difficult...)

Going out early in the morning,
you get into a box on the rope:
Coming out late in the evening,
you get into another box on the rope.
(Closed-circuit cameras watch the customers, operating
  automatically.)
As yet, no one has gotten out
of line (the police carry loaded guns, in a state of alert).
Whatever the line,
to violate it means to be excluded, to be pushed out,
to be expelled, and you will be opposed
(you crawl on the line on all fours).

그런데 너는 가끔
어제 오후에도 불쑥 이렇게 묻는다,
꼭 이렇게 살아야만 되는 건가?
산다는 것이 꼭 이것뿐인가?
그러자
갑자기 괄호가 열리면서
금 밖의 바깥이
이름 붙일 수 없는
하얀 조명을 콸콸 쏟고 있는 느낌이 들면서
바깥—미지—미래로 연결되는 격렬한
아름다운 밀물이
괄호 안의 세상을 수몰시키며
나를 괄호 밖으로
밖으로 둥둥 방류시키는 것이었다,

무엇이 이 괄호 안에
나를 유폐시키고 있는가?
이 괄호 안에 내가 있어야만
안전한 사람들은 누구인가?
괄호에 의해 전적으로 유지되는
이 낡은 지평선
밑에 있는

But you often—
you did even yesterday afternoon—ask,
Must one live like this?
Is this all there is to life?
Just then,
suddenly, the parentheses open
and from beyond the line
an unnameable
white light rushes in,

and a violent, beautiful tide from
the outside, from an unknown future,
sinks the world within the parentheses
and carries me
to the outside where I float, buoyantly adrift.

What seals me
within these parentheses?
Who is it that is secure
only when I am within these parentheses?
What is it? Who is it? Why this fascism of desire
below this old horizon

그것, 그이, 그분의 욕망의 파시즘은

무엇인가?

that is held up wholly

by these parentheses?

유목을 위하여 · 5

—줄어드는 나

나는 점점 줄어든다,
어제 입었던 옷이 헐렁거린다,
나는 늘 줄어든다,
어제 살았던 괄호가
오늘은 너무 커서
허수아비 누더기처럼 펄렁거린다,

내가 줄어드는 그만큼
세상은 늘 넓어져 간다,
나는 늘 보잘것없이 줄어들고
세상은 점령자가 늘 그렇게
늘어만 가는 것이다,
(그러니까 나는 세계의 내면화에
실패했다는 것이 아닌가?
릴케는 내면말고는 어느 곳에도
세상은 없노니…… 라고
말했는데)

나날이 줄어드느라
입을 옷이 없어진다,
대학 때 입던 옷은
곡두귀신이 뒤집어 쓰는 푸새자루처럼

For Nomads · 5

—Shrinking I

Little by little I am shrinking.
The clothes I wore yesterday are too loose.
I am forever shrinking.
The parentheses I lived in yesterday
are too far apart today
and they wave like rags on a scarecrow.

The world is constantly enlarging
by the same amount that I shrink.
I am always shrinking so insignificantly,
and the world is always increasing
its territory.
(Doesn't this mean that I have failed
to interiorize the world?
Rilke said that there is no world
except the interior....)

Because I shrink daily,
I have no more clothes to wear.
The clothes I used to wear in my college days
are quite loose,
like the gunny sack that the grain spirit would toss over its

제일 헐렁하고
여학교 때 입던 옷
국민학교 일학년 때 입던 옷도
적어도 지금의 나보다는 컸던 것이다.
(역사 이래로 이렇게 좁은 절망의 궁지만이
자신의 유일한 둥지인
그런 동물이 있었는지 없었는지)

강보에 싸여 있던 배냇저고리의
영토 속으로 들어가 본다,
아무것도 가리지 못했던
배꼽만한 옷,
바람과 비누방울의 영혼들과
짝을 이룬 포근포근한
숨결,
나에서 당신으로의 한이 없는
따스한 향기,

봄 여름 가을 겨울
나는 누더기들을 버린다,
봄 여름 가을 겨울
누더기를 버리는 날은

head,*

and the clothes that I wore in high school
and even those that I wore in the first grade
are at the least all larger than I am now.
(I wonder if any animals in history were ever
in such a tight spot of despair
for their only nest.)

I enter the territory
swaddled in a baby blanket,
a garment the size of a belly button,
that could hardly cover anything,
a baby' s breath matching
the souls of the wind and of soap bubbles,
an infinite, warm fragrance
from me to you,
in the spring, summer, fall, and winter.
I throw away my rags
in the spring, summer, fall, and winter.
The day I throw away my rags is
the day I wish to throw away anything of myself that resembles
a rag,

누더기 같은 온갖 나를 버리고 싶은 날이다,
봄 여름 가을 겨울
누더기 같은 나를 버리는 날은
나를 점령하고 있는 세상의
피억류자들을 풀어버리고
저기 저 날아가는 나비,
구름처럼 사라지는
장미꽃 위의 이슬 속으로
가벼이 아주 가벼이
작게 아주 작게 환생하고 싶은
끝나지 않은 꿈 때문인지도 모른다.

in the spring, summer, fall, and winter.

The day I discard myself, my rag-like self,

is the day I untie the oppressed of the world that fill me

and, like that butterfly flying over there—

or perhaps it is an unfinished dream

wanting to be reborn—

however lightly,

however tiny—

into dew drops on a rose that vanish

as do the clouds.

---

*Allusion uncertain. Tr.

유목을 위하여 · 6

–상복을 입은 나비

하얀 배추흰나비 한 마리가
개집 지붕 위로
고요히 날아간다,
루키는 놀라서 멍멍 짖어본다,
멍멍 짖다가 도둑 같은 건 아니군
하는 듯
앞발을 들고
허공에 반원을 그리면서
그것을 잡아보려고 한다,
아마 먹을 것인 줄 알고
잡아먹으려고 하는 것인가……?
끈에 묶인 루키의 앞발이
허공 중에 잠시 멈춰
미세하게 떨고 있다,
(짐승의 앞발이 그만큼 대지에서
멀리 떨어진 것을
나는 처음 보았다)

눈부신 햇살 속에서
멍멍하게 깨어난 나는
방금 무언가 경이로운 것을 본 것 같다,
루키야, 너는 지금 도를

For Nomads · 6

—Butterfly in Mourning Clothes

A white cabbage butterfly
silently flutters
over the roof of the dog house.
Rookie is frightened and begins to bark,
but stops, thinking it wasn' t
a thief.
He raises his paws,
tracing an arc in the air,
and tries to catch it.
Does he want to catch
and eat it...?
Rookie' s paws, held back by the rope,
stop momentarily in the air
and tremble slightly.
(I have never seen an animal' s paws separated so far
above the earth.)

Waking up like a moron
in the brilliant sunlight,
I have just witnessed something of a wonder!
Rookie! You have just performed
an act of enlightenment!

행한 것이다,
아름다운 무한에 닿으려고 할 때
우리는 그런 난생 처음 해보는
무상의 무용에
잠시 자신의 모든 것을 고요히 내맡기게
되는 것이다,
(나비 한 마리보다 더 큰
도둑이 어디 있으리)

그런 때 우리는 말뚝을 잊어버린다,
중력의 말뚝,
무거운 땅 속으로 우리를 캄캄하게
끌어당기는
뿌리혹박테리아처럼 주렁주렁 매달리는
죽음의 인력을
우리는 잠시 잊어버리며
네 옆에 놓인 밥그릇과
모가지의 패찰과 쇠사슬들을
고요히 놓아주고 만다,

하얀 배추흰나비 한 마리가 날아간다,
이런 아름다운 나비가

When we want to reach for beautiful infinity,
we calmly give our whole self
to the most gratuitous dance
we have ever performed in our lives.
(Where would there be a greater thief than a single butterfly?!)

At such times, we forget the tethering post,
and its gravitational pull.
We forget the pull of death, like
root bacteria that cling in clusters like bulbous fruit,
which pulls down into the dark, dense ground, and
we silently let go of
the bowls next to us,
of the tags around our necks,
and of the chains of steel.

A white cabbage butterfly flies by.
The existence of such a butterfly in our lives
suggests that there is a way to
tear down this wall which locks us in, and to get out.
God is infinitely raising us
from the outside

우리의 생 속에 있는 것은
가두어진 담을 허물고
바깥으로 나가는 길이 어디엔가 있음을
암시하는 것이다.
신이 너를 바깥에서
무한히 들어올려주려고
기다리고 있는 것이다,

하루 속에
하늘을 누각하는 나비,
막힌 창호를 뚫고
나를 구명하려고
번쩍이는 깜박이는
조용한 대형나비들

and is waiting.

A butterfly etches the sky
in the daylight,
breaking through the paper barrier of the window,
a quiet, giant butterfly,
glistening and twinkling,
comes to rescue me.

진주 기르기 · 1

심야에, 멍청히,
제시카의 추리극장을 보며
누워 있는데
긴급한 파발마 글씨로
하얀 자락이 달려간다.
RH마이너스 B형 혈액을 급히 찾습니다 신촌 세브란스
병원 392의 0161 응급실로 빨리……

나는 RH마이너스 혈액이
없어서
그냥 누워서 양파링을 바삭바삭
먹으며
TV를 본다.

누가 나를 불렀나?
유리창에 가득찬 밤이
내 얼굴을 쳐다보는 것 같아
등을 돌리고 누우며
홀로 한번 더 말해 본다
나 · 는 · R · H · 마 · 이 · 너 · 스 · 피 · 가 · 아 · 닌 · 데 · 뭘……

그렇게
80년대는 저물고

Growing Pearl · 1

In the deep of the night, as I lie vacantly
watching Jessica's Mystery Theater,
urgent lettering, a white ribbon, runs across:
"RH negative B-type blood
urgently sought, contact the emergency room,
Shinchon Severance Hospital, 392-0161,
immediately."

I don't have RH negative blood.
I'm lying here munching onion rings
and watching TV.

Did someone call me?
The night, which fills the window,
seems to be staring me in the face.
I turn my back.
I say once more to myself.
I am not R H Ne-ga-tive so why...?

Thus
the Eighties came to a close,
and I, who never lost a drop of blood,
who never gave a drop of blood to these times—

피 한방울 손해보지 않은 나는
그 시대에 피 한방울 보태지 않은 나는
양파링처럼 너무도 유순하게
누군가의 깊은 목구멍 속으로
자꾸만 녹아들어가고 있는 느낌이다.

이렇게 녹아버려도 좋은 것일까
이렇게 삼켜져도 되는 것일까
몸 속에 자꾸만 돌이 쌓여가는 기분으로
잠들었다가
(목구멍까지 돌이 차오르면
우린 행복하게도 잠수성공 익사성공
을 이룰 수도 있었을 텐데)

아, 안돼, 잠옷 같은 수의를 떨치고
바람 같은 신발을 신고
어둠의 눈물 묻은 대문을 나서며
나는 신촌 세브란스 병원이 있다는
새벽의 방향으로
푸르게 푸르게 달리기 시작한다.
내 비록
R · H · 마 · 이 · 너 · 스 · B · 형 · 피 · 는 · 없 · 지 · 만……

like onion rings all too willingly,
I feel myself dissolving again and again
into the depths of someone's throat.

Is it good to be dissolved like this?
Is it all right to be swallowed up like this?
I am falling asleep, as if rocks were piling up inside my body.
(If they reached my throat, I could have happily
brought on submersion and death by drowning.)

Oh, no. Shedding my shroud-like nightgowns,
putting on shoes like the wind,
going out the door stained by tears of darkness,
I begin running, green, ever so green,
toward the dawn and Shinchon Severance Hospital:
even if I
do not have R H Ne-ga-tive B type blood....

창문을 닫고 블라인드를 내리고
커튼을 치고 이불 속에 누워봐도

어떻게든 세상은 쳐들어온다.

제목만 길고 내용은 없는 이 시처럼

세상이 다 나를 살아주고
나는 종속절처럼 점령된 몇 마디 말을
그저 덧붙일 수 있을 뿐이다.

이미 녹즙기 스위치 ON이 눌러져
혼비백산의 회전이 상당히 진행되어온 것이다.

어디에 가서 이 생을 구하리오.
삭발처럼 이 세상을 잘라내버리고
어디에 가서 피랍의 문을 어떻게 쳐부수리오?

Windows Closed, Blinds Down, Curtains Drawn, Comforter Pulled over Me

The world invades no matter what.

Like this poem with long title and no content,
the world will live for me
and I can only add
a few words, occupying it like a subordinate clause.

Already the juicer has been pushed "on," and the whirling
of the "It'll-scare-the-wits-out-of-you" has been going on for
quite some time.

Where can I go to save my life?
Cutting loose from this world, shearing my head,*
where can I go and how can I break down the door of my
captivity?

* "Shearing one's head" is a metonym for "becoming a Buddhist monk." Tr.

넝마의 운율

벽을 보아도 이젠 목을 매달 생각을 하지 않는다. 예전엔 벽 앞에 오래 앉아 있으면 어디에 못을 박고 목을 매달까 그런 생각을 했는데…… 〈잃어버린 시간을 찾아서〉 그런 류의 길을 가는 사람을 부러워한다. 그런 사람에겐 시간이 무척 따스하고 행복할 것 같다. 어느 시간을 열어야 못자욱 없는 벽을 만날 수 있을까?

*

배추흰나비 한 마리가
엉겅퀴꽃 뒤에서
날아간다
이 세상 어딘가에 행복이 있을 것만 같은
소식이다
가슴에 눈물을 많이 모은
알들만이
그런 엄청난 시위를 할 수 있다
헌 신문지 같은
지상의 누더기들을 슬고
저렇게 눈부신 人肉의 퇴원을 해보았으면!

*

The Rhythm of Rags

Now I don't think about hanging myself when I look at the wall. In the old days I used to think about pounding in a nail and hanging myself when I sat in front of the wall for a long time... "Remembrance of things past": I envy people who go after such things. To them, it seems, time is so cozy and happy. Which times should I look into, to find a wall without the trace of a nail?

A lone white cabbage butterfly
flies behind a thistle flower.
It is news that somewhere in this world
there must be happiness.
Only eggs that have gathered so many tears
in their heart
can put on such a grand display.
To get rid of the rags of the earth
that look like old newspapers:
if only I could be discharged from the hospital with such dazzling human flesh!

You used to tell me,
when you were separating laundry wrung out by the washing

세탁기 속에서
탈수된 빨래들을 정리하다가
양말과 손수건이 부둥켜 안고 있는 것을
보면 죽고 싶다고 넌 나에게 말했지,
넌 그러니? 아, 어쩌면, 넌, 정말……

난, 글쎄, 난, 말이야,
그런 것을 보면
이 세상 어딘가에 아직 사랑이 남아 있는
것을 믿게 되고,
쓰레기가 쓰레기에게 친절하게 굴 듯이
삶에게 마구 달려들어
삐약삐약거리고 싶구나, 글쎄……

*

벽 위에 남은 희미한 못자욱들. 지워지지 않는다. 별똥무늬 달려와 박힌 누전의 뜸처럼. 그렇게 별들과 사랑을 나누었던 사람도 있구나. 못을 박으며 그리움의 벼락에 구멍 숭숭 뚫린 넝마 한 장의 모습으로 별들의 수로를 이곳에 내려던 사람아. 그러니까 넌 지금껏 벽에 의해 살아온 것이다. 그러므로 넌 지금껏 별에 의해 살아온 것이다. 오 그렇지 않은가?

machine,

that you felt like dying whenever you saw a sock and a handkerchief tangled in an embrace.

What? How you are so truly....

I'm, well, I'm... I'll tell you:

when I see such things,

I believe

love still remains somewhere in the world.

Rubbish being kind to rubbish,

I just want to lunge into life

and chirp, like....

Faint traces of nails on the wall—Do not erase them!—like the moxa marks of an electrical burn, like the etching of a shooting star, there were some who shared their love with the stars. Pounding the nails with a rag riddled with punctures made by the thunder of longing, you were trying to build a canal for the stars. You have lived up to now held by the stars. Oh, isn' t it true?!

나는 쇼핑한다 고로 나는 존재한다

페르시아 만에서 전쟁이 터지자마자
TV들은 모조리 전쟁생방송 체제로
돌입하였다.
올림픽보다도 세계 권투 헤비급 타이틀
매치보다도
더 많은 시청률을 올려주며
시청자들은 사막 위 폭풍을 바라보았다.

한밤중에 이루어진 다국적군의 바그다드
시가 공습에 대해 한 기자는
〈미국 독립기념일의 불꽃놀이를 일백 배 확대한 것 같다〉고
말했고,
미 ABC TV의 앵커맨 피터 제닝스는
〈이것은 멋대로 진행되는 쇼〉라고
토를 달았다.
한국의 한 증권사 객장에서는
〈막상 전쟁이 터지고나니 후련합니다.
전쟁이 단기간에 끝날 것이라는 확신 때문인지
주가가 폭등해 얼마나 다행인지
모르겠어요〉
라면서 투자자들은 오히려 전쟁을
즐기는 것 같았다. (1991년 1월 19일자 동아일보 중에서)

I Shop, Therefore I Am

As soon as war broke out in the Persian Gulf,
all television switched to live-reporting
of the war, over their broadcasting systems.
More than they did the Olympic Games and heavy-weight title
boxing matches, which
raised the ratings,
viewers watched the storms on the desert.

In regard to the bombing raids
made during the night
by the multinational coalition force
over the city of Baghdad,
a reporter said,
"It was a hundred times better than fireworks on the 4th of July,"
and anchorman Peter Jennings of ABC added,
"This is a show performed without a script."
At one Korean stock market, a man in the gallery commented,
"Now that the war is really on, I feel relieved.
Because the war was supposed to be finished in a short time,
stock prices soared. What a relief!"
Investors were rather

엄청난 인명의 살상이라는
대학살의 느낌은 없고
불꽃놀이 생방송과 주가가 폭등과
앵커맨이 영웅이 되는
찬란한 쇼가 있을 뿐이었다.

나는 인간의 모습을 딱 두 번 보았다.
방독 마스크를 쓴 엄마가
우주인 같은 모습으로
병원의 비닐보호막 속에 누워 있는 환자 아기를
들여다보는 장면이었다.
슬퍼하는 여인과 아픈 아기의 눈동자는
서로 부딪치며 이런 최후의 암호를
주고받는 듯했다.
— 인간은 이제 이 세계의 중심명제가 아니지요,
그렇지요? 호모 사피엔스 여러분?

그리고 쇼핑을 하려고 세계각국의
백화점마다 슈퍼마켓마다 벼룩시장마다
현찰을 든 손들이
달려가고 있다.
비싸게 팔리고자 하는 욕망과

enjoying the war. (*Don-A Daily News*, Jan. 19, 1991)

There was no sense of massive slaughter,
of the killing of an incredible number of human beings,
but only of a glorious show of fireworks, broadcast live,
of stock prices soaring.
and of anchormen becoming heroes.

I have seen a truly human face only twice.
The scene was, a mother wearing a gas mask,
looking like some astronaut,
looking at her baby inside a plastic shelter in a hospital.
The sad woman's eyes and her baby's pain-filled eyes
met and seemed to exchange a last
secret code.

—The human being is no longer the central theme of this world, is it, you dear *homo sapiens*?

And in order to shop,
cash in hand,
they run to every department store, to every supermarket, to

값싸게 사들이고자 하는 욕망 사이에서
헐리우드 쇼보다 더 재미있는 쇼는
시시각각 진행되고
비닐 위에 사진 실크스크린 된 것 같은
인간의 형체 비슷한 뭉그러진 모습들이
이리저리
나는 쇼핑한다 고로 나는 존재한다고
욕망의 질주로 부윰하게 떠오르고 있는
몽중보행이여.

every flea market,
all over the world.
Between the desire to sell high
and the desire to buy low,
a show more entertaining than Hollywood
is performed every second,
and disfigured human shapes,
silk-screened onto plastic wrap,
jostle this way and that.

I shop, therefore I am:
a sleepwalking arising
en masse in a mad dash of desire.

떠도는 환유 · 1

몇 마장인지 알지 못할
장마비가 연일연일 내리고 있다,
창이 좁아서인지
세상이 위태하리만치 어두워진다,
어둡고 긴, 무슨 포식의,
동물 창자 속으로
끌려 들어가는 듯.
—여보세요, 여보세요,
여긴 너무 어두워요, 말 좀 해봐요,
—말하면 뭘하니, 넌 날 볼 수가 없잖아.
—그래도 괜찮아요, 말하면 밝아질 테니까요.

*

세상엔 벽이 되려는 창과 싸우는 사람과
창이 되려는 벽과 싸우는 사람,
그렇게 두 진영의 사람이 있다,

그런 사람들은 모두 세상을 자택인 듯이
살고 있는 것 같다,

나, 나, 나라는 나가비는

Floating Metonymy · 1

Day after day the rain has been falling
far and wide.
A slit of a window has made
the world dark and dangerous
as I am drawn into
the long, dark intestines of the beast
of gluttony.
—Hello? Hello?
It's so dark. Please say something.
—What's the use? You can't see me anyway.
—That's O.K. If you said something, it would get lighter.

*

There are two camps of people:
the people who fight the window that would become a wall,
and those who fight the wall that would become a window.

These are the people who live in this world
as if it is home.

As for me, a wanderer, I

영구 임대주택인 듯이, 아니, 아니,
임시 임대주택인 듯이 生을 대하며
조만간 흘러가 버리고 말 것 같다,
너무 쉽게 흘러가 주는 것은 아닐까?

가끔씩 조명이 너무 어둡다고
투덜대기나 하면서……
위조여권 같은 말을 따라서
출렁출렁…… 글썽글썽……

face life as if it were permanent, rental housing—no, no,
rather temporary, rental housing—
Am I flowing away all too easily?

Occasionally, grumbling that the lighting
is too dark···
and following words, counterfeit passports,
I flow along among the lapping waves, my eyes brimming
with tears....

떠도는 환유 · 3
—이웃집 여자들

가슴 속에 꽃잎이 지고 있다,
꽃잎이 지고 있다,
지는 꽃잎은 지려므나,
누가 그 안에서 울고 있는지도 모른다,

가슴 속으로 불나방이 뛰어들고 있다,
불나방이 뛰어들고 있다,
불이 그리운 불나방아
내 가슴 속에 아직도 무슨 촛불이 타고 있다고
그러느냐, 그러느냐

가슴 속에 지붕이 흔들리고 있다,
지붕이 흔들리고 있다,
누가 그 천장 위에서 드르렁 드르렁
코를 골며 아직도 자고 있는지도
모른다,

산다는 것은 언제나
그렇게도 많은 나를 데리고
선인장이 양쪽으로 빽빽하게 심겨진
가시통로의 좁은 길을
우왕좌왕 찔리면서 걸어간다는 것이었다,

Floating Metonymy · 3

—Women in the Neighborhood

Flower petals are falling in my heart.
Petals are falling.
Falling petals fall and fall.
Someone may be crying there.

A moth springs into my heart.
A moth springs inside.
A moth longing for the flame:
what do you see still aflame in my heart
that you spring in, again and again?

A roof is shaking in my heart.
A roof is shaking.
Someone may be asleep
upstairs, snoring
away, sound asleep.

In living, I am always led
(so many of me)
on foot, poked left and right,
through a narrow, thorny passage
lined with thickly planted cacti.

다만 피를 보고싶지는 않다는
심정뿐이었다, 뿐이었다.

피를 보고싶지는 않아서
와글와글, 바글바글, 드르렁 드르렁
엉엉, 흑흑……
이런 시끄러운 나를 데리고
〈짜깁기 전문〉 이런 간판이 붙은
옷 수선소 앞을 지나가면
꼭 나를 닮은 엉성한 얼굴의 여자 하나가
들들들 들들들……
손재봉틀을 열심히 돌리며
얼굴을 숙이고 부지런히, 이런 어수선한
넝마 누더기를 꿰어맞추는 모습도 보인다

Wanting to avoid seeing blood
whenever I direct my noisy person—
I talk, boil over, snore,
weep, sob—
along the street and pass the seamstress
with her sign "Reweaving a Specialty,"
I always see a woman with a non-descript face like my own,
running her chugging sewing machine by hand.
Her head is bent down and she diligently
pieces together her rags
all in disarray.

떠도는 환유 · 5

—무어라고 불러야 좋을까

사랑도, 눈물도, 진짜가 아닌 것 같애,
사랑 비슷한
눈물 비슷한
흔적 비슷한
분노 비슷한
그런 비슷한 것들이 나 비슷한 것들을
감싸고
한 줄기 햇빛의 선 속에 우우 우우
갇혀 떠도는 먼지처럼
생 비슷한 것들을 이루고 있어

나 비슷한 것들아
시대 비슷한
나라 비슷한
지식인 비슷한
고뇌 비슷한
외침 비슷한
절망도 낙천도 아닌
어스름 비슷한
이 향방의 묘혈 속에서
죽음 비슷한 生이 있어
살지도 죽지도 못하고

Floating Metonymy · 5

—What Should I Call This?

Even love, tears, don' t seem real.
Something like love,
something like tears,
something like scars,
something like rage—
such things, semblances,
envelope the thing
resembling me;
in the sunlight,
milling about,
like roaming particles of trapped dust,
we form something like a life.

All of them are like me—
in something of an era,
in something of a country,
being something of an intellectual,
having something of suffering,
making something of a scream.
With neither despair nor optimism,
in near darkness,
in this tomb of my whereabouts,

엄마 비슷한
아내 비슷한
자식 비슷한
교수 비슷한
시인 비슷한 것들을
배우 비슷하게
은막 비슷한 곳에서

너, 참, 정말, 무엇에 널 걸 거니?, 응?, 말해봐,
참, 무엇에든 널 걸어야 할 거 아냐?
이런 닭달 속에서도, 아무데도 날 걸지 않는,

아무데도 걸 수가 없는, 걸 것이 없는, 파쇄된
나를, 아니 나 비슷한 것들을 데리고,
사전꾼처럼 사기꾼, 아니 무한히 높은 곳에서
밀어버려 무한낙하로 산산이 엎어지고 있는
사닥다리의 해방처럼……

there is life that resembles death.

I can neither live nor die —
something of a mom,
something of a wife,
something of a child,
something of a professor,
something-or-other of a poet,
something like an actor;
somewhere, as on a silver screen.

"You! Really, truly, what are you going
to hang onto? Huh? Tell me!
Really, don't you have to hang onto something?"
Pestered, I did not hang myself onto anything:
there was nowhere I could hang onto,
nothing even to hang.
Broken, I—no, I led all those who are like me,
like a loan shark, a crook—no, from an infinitely high place
I pushed them out into an infinite descent,
like the liberation of a ladder
tumbling down, the pieces scattering....

세상에서 가장 무거운 싸움

The Heaviest of Struggles in the World

세상에서 가장 무거운 싸움 · 1

「이 문은 자동도어이오니
개폐를 운전자에게 맡겨주십시오」

누군가 나에게 넥타이를 입힌다
그리고 질질 끌고 간다

The Heaviest of Struggles in the World · 1

"This door is automatic.
Let the driver operate it."

Someone puts a collar on me,
and drags me along.

세상에서 가장 무거운 싸움 · 2

아침에 눈뜨면 세계가 있다,
아침에 눈뜨면 당연의 세계가 있다,
당연의 세계는 당연히 있다,
당연의 세계는 당연히 거기에 있다,

당연의 세계는 왜, 거기에,
당연히 있어야 할 곳에 있는 것처럼,
왜, 맨날, 당연히, 거기에 있는 것일까,
당연의 세계는 거기에 너무도 당연히 있어서
그 두꺼운 껍질을 벗겨보지도 못하고
당연히 거기에 존재하고 있다

당연의 세계는 누가 만들었을까,
당연의 세계는 당연히 당연한 사람이 만들었겠지,
당연히 그것을 만들 만한 사람,
그것을 만들어도 당연한 사람,

그러므로, 당연의 세계는 물론 옳다,
당연은 언제나 물론 옳기 때문에
당연의 세계의 껍질을 벗기려다가는
물론의 손에 맞고 쫓겨난다,
당연한 손은 보이지 않는 손이면서

The Heaviest of Struggles in the World · 2

When I wake up in the morning, the world is there;
when I wake up in the morning, the World of Propriety* is there.
The World of Propriety properly exists,
and the World of Propriety is properly there.

Why is the World of Propriety always there,
as if where it should properly be?
The World of Propriety is there so properly
that no one can peel away its thick skin:
it is properly there.

Who created the World of Propriety?
The World of Propriety must have been created by proper people,
people who are capable of creating it properly,
people who would be proper even if they did create it.

Therefore, the World of Propriety is, of course, right.
Because Propriety is always right, of course.
If you were to peel away the skin of the World of Propriety,
you would be hit by the hand of Of Course and be kicked out.
The hands of Propriets are invible hands, and
yet why are they so properly the hands of Of Course?

왜 그렇게 당연한 물론의 손일까,

당연한 세계에서 나만 당연하지 못하여
당연의 세계가 항상 낯선 나는
물론의 세계의 말을 또한 믿을 수가 없다,
물론의 세계 또한
정녕 나를 좋아하진 않겠지

당연의 세계는 물론의 세계를 길들이고
물론의 세계는 우리의 세계를 길들이고 있다,
당연의 세계에 소송을 걸어라
물론의 세계에 소송을 걸어라
나날이 다가오는 모래의 점령군,
하루종일 발이 푹푹 빠지는 당연의 세계를
생사불명, 힘들여 걸어오면서, 세상에서 가장 무거운 싸움은
그와의 싸움임을 알았다
물론의 모래가 콘크리트로 굳기 전에
당연의 감옥이 온 세상 끝까지 먹어치우기 전에
당연과 물론을 양손에 들고
아삭아삭 내가 먼저 뜯어먹었으면.

In the World of Propriety, I am the only one who is not proper.
I am forever unfamiliar with the World of Propriety
and cannot trust the words of the World of Of Course either.
The world of Of course, does not
like me at all.

The World of Propriety tames the World of Of Course,
and the World of Of Course tames our world.
Sue the World of Propriety!
Sue the World of Of Course!
The occupying force of sand comes nearer, day by day,
the World of Propriety into which our feet sink all day long.
Not knowing whether we are dead or alive, we trudge with
all our might,
for the heaviest battle in the world is to fight against it.
Before the sand of Of Course sets in concrete
and the prison of Propriety swallows the whole world,
I wish I could hold Propriety and Of Course in my hands
and gobble them up! Chomp! Chomp!

---

* Propriety here refers to "as a matter of course," "the unquestionable common sense" or "the accepted order of things." cf. "Rightfulness" by Bro. Anthony Teague. Tr.

솟구쳐 오르기 · 1

억압을 뚫지 않으면
억압을
억압을
억압을

악업이 되어
악업이
악업이
악업이

두려우리라

절벽 모서리에 뜀틀을 짓고
절벽의 모서리에 뜀틀을 짓고
내 옆구리를 찌른 창을 장대로 삼아
하늘 높이
장대 높이뛰기를 해보았으면

눈썹이 푸른 하늘에 닿을 때까지
푸른 하늘에 속눈썹이 젖을 때까지

Soaring · 1

If we do not break out of our oppression,
of our oppression...
of our oppression...
of our oppression,

it will become our sin,
our sin...
our sin...
our sin;

and we will be afraid.

Build a trampoline at the edge of a cliff,
build a trampoline at the edge of a cliff;
make a pole out of the spear that has pierced my side—
I wish I could vault
high up into the sky

until my eyebrows touch the blue,
until my eyelashes soak in the blue.

Ah, isn't life a longing

아, 삶이란 그런 장대 높이뛰기의 날개를
원하는 것이 아닐까,
상처의 그물을 피할 수도 없지만
상처의 그물 아래 갇혀 살 수도 없어

내 옆구리를 찌른 창을 장대로 삼아
장대 높이뛰기를 해보았으면
억압을 악업을
그렇게 솟아올라
아, 한번 푸르게 물리칠 수 있다면

for the wings of a pole vault?
We can' t avoid a web of wounds,
but neither can we live our life imprisoned by this web of
wounds.

I wish I could pole-vault
with the spear that has pierced my side
so high up
as to conquer, if only for once, oppression and sin
and be victorious.

솟구쳐 오르기 · 2

상처의 용수철
그것이 우리를 날게 하지 않으면
상처의 용수철
그것이 우리를 솟구쳐 오르게 하지 않으면

파란 싹이 검은 땅에서 솟아오르는 것이나
무섭도록 붉은 황토밭 속에서 파아란 보리가
씩씩하게 솟아올라 봄바람에 출렁출렁 흔들리는 것이나
힘없는 개구리가 바위 밑에서
자그만 폭약처럼 튀어나가는 것이나
빨간 넝쿨장미가 아파아파 가시를 딛고
불타는 듯이 담벼락을 기어 올라가는 것이나
민들레가 엉엉 울며 시멘트 조각을 밀어내는 것이나
검은 나뭇가지 어느새 봄이 와
그렁그렁 눈물 같은 녹색의 바다를 일으키는 것이나

상처의 용수철이 없다면
삶은 무게에 짓뭉그러진 나비알
상처의 용수철이 없다면
존재는
무서운 사과 한 알의 원죄의 감금일 뿐
죄와 벌의 화농일 뿐

Soaring · 2

The coil spring of our wounds—
if it doesn' t make us fly...
The coil spring of our wounds—
if it doesn' t make us soar...

A green bud sprouts from the dark soil;
green barley bravely rises in a field of dreadfully red clay
and waves in the spring breeze;
a meek little frog darts like a bullet under a rock;
red roses endure the pain of their thorny branches,
climbing a wall as if on fire;
a dandelion, wailing, pushes aside bits of concrete;
spring comes suddenly to dark branches
and creates a sea of green like welling tear drops.

If there were no coil spring of our wounds,
life would be a butterfly egg crushed under its weight.
If there were no coil spring of our wounds,
our being
would only be an imprisonment in original sin,
brought about by the fearsome apple;
would only be a festering of crime and punishment.

솟구쳐 오르기 · 5

진실로 무서운 것은
우리 머리 위의 그물이 아니다
밖에 있는 그물이 아니다
현대인의 핏속에 DNA처럼 입력되어 있는
무기력, 망각, 순응의 유전자 지문들

그 그물의 식민통치를 뿌리치지 않고
어떻게 솟아오르기를 바랄 것인가?
가장 야만스러운 열정이여
나에게 와 다오
가장 야만스러운 정열
잔혹한 그 검은 웃음이 없다면
누가 우리를 그물에서 해방시킬 것인가?

—누군가는 그 학살에 책임을 져야 한다
—누가 그 뺑소니 차량을 보신 분이 있습니까?
1980년 5월 18일 연희동 네거리에서
수백 명의 어린아이들이 뺑소니차에 치여 숨졌습니다
그, 극악무도한, 가증스러운
뺑소니 차량 목격하신 분 안 계십니까?
이런 현수막이 쳐진 거리
시간이 가도 현수막이

Soaring · 5

The truly frightful thing
is not the net cast over our heads.
It's not the net outside.
It's the fingerprints of the genes of lethargy, oblivion,
   acquiescence,
stored in modern man's blood like DNA.

How can we expect to rise up
without tearing away the colonial rule of the net?
Most primal passion,
please come to me!
Without that most barbarous passion,
without that horrific dark smile,
who will free us from the net?

—Someone must take responsibility for the slaughter!
—Isn't there someone who saw the runaway car?
On May 18th, 1980, at the intersection of Yon-Hee Dong,
several hundred children were killed by hit-and-run cars.
Isn't there anyone who witnessed these vicious, deplorable,
hit-and-run vehicles?
Streets are hung with placards bearing these kinds of

내려지지 않는 거리

잘못이라는 단어는 언제나
나의 뇌리에 틀어박혀 있다
죄라는 단어도 언제나
나의 뇌리에 틀어박혀 있다
심판이라는 단어도 언제나
나의 뇌리에 틀어박혀 있다

우리는 모두 목격을 하였다, 목격을 하긴
한 것이다,
목격자의 원죄, 목격자의 비굴, 목격자의 공포가
지상의 인간들의 날개를 찢고 있다,
깃털을 흩트리고 있다,

목격이 원죄를 형성해 버린 이 땅에서
우리 모두 원죄를 벗기 위해서는
보내라, 보내라,
가야 할 것들을 종말처리장으로 보내고,
죄가 경미한 사람들은 시청 앞 분수대에서
공개목욕을 시키자
공개목욕을 시키자

questions,
streets from which the placards have not been removed,
even as time passes.

The word mistake
is always stuck in my head.
The word sin also is always
stuck in my head.
We all witnessed it. We were witnesses.
The original sin of witnesses, the cowardice of witnesses, the
terror of witnesses
are tearing off the wings of men on earth.
They scatter their feathers.

In this land where witnessing amounts to original sin,
to be free from original sin, one has to
send, send,
send away everything that must go to the last treatment center.
For those whose crimes are light,
let's give them a public bathing,
let's give them a public bathing
in the fountain at the city-hall plaza.

메아리 없는 거리에선
오렌지가 주렁주렁 익어가고
사이비가 사바사바 자라나고
성수대교가 무너진다, 무너진다, 무너진다.

While oranges* are ripening in clusters,
and sham is growing in the midst of bribery
on the street where there is no echo,
Great Seong-Soo Bridge is falling down, falling down,
falling down.

* Reference to "O-ren-ji-jok"(lit. orange-tribe); A term created in the 1990s to refer to young people, generally fromaffluent families, who were into conspicuous consumption and fast living. Tr.

솟구쳐 오르기 · 8

—나는 웃는다

나의 웃음은 오래된, 아주 오래된
웃음이었다,
태초에 혼돈이 있었을 때부터
그 혼돈과 행복하게 반죽되었던 나의 웃음은
최초의 상처로 우주가 갈라질 때
세상 가장자리로 밀쳐져 대롱대롱 매달려 있으면서부터
시작된, 벼랑을 뒤덮어버릴 웃음으로,
세상의 모든 밤 속에서 웃고 있었는지도 모른다

나의 웃음은 바람이 부는 동안
흔들리는 잎새들의 쓰라림과 원통이었다가
밀물이 들어올 때 빠져나가는
세상의 모든 썰물들의 도주의 웃음소리인지도 모른다

뉴욕 5번가 지하철역에서
지하철을 기다리고 있을 때
내 옆에 서 있던 한 여자가 갑자기 웃기 시작했지,
그르렁그르렁 가래 끓는 소리 같기도 하고
쿨럭쿨럭 기침 토하는 소리 같기도 한 웃음소리는
지하동굴에 가득 찬 저녁의 무거운 숙명과
삶에 지친 울음이 반죽된, 희망 없는 우울의 둔주곡인지도,
어깨는 파도치고, 얼굴을 가린 손가락새로

Soaring · 8

—I Laugh

My laughter was an ancient, a very ancient,
laughter:
from the beginning of time, in chaos,
laughter that mixed happily in that confusion.
When the universe was split open by the very first wound,
when I was pushed to the edge of the world and dangled
precariously,
my laughing began, with a laughter that will cover the abyss.
I might have been laughing at all the nights of this world.

My laughter might have been the pain and the suffering
of the leaves that are blown in the wind,
and it might have been the sound of the flight
of every low tide in the world before an advancing high tide.

At the subway station on Fifth Avenue in New York,
I was waiting for the train.
A woman standing by me suddenly began to laugh.
It sounded like a congested wheezing full of phlegm;
it sounded like coughing.
The heavy fate of the evening filled the underground cavern
and mixed with the cry of a tired life from between her

악령의 뜨거운 희열이 넘쳐흐르고 있었는지도,

지하철이 뿌연 빛을 비추며 들어오고 있을 때
그녀는 땅 아래로 몸을 날려, 떨어져
죽고 말았어, 웃으면서, 선로 위에서
지하철의 무게로 삶을 마감한 그녀는 흥건한 피와
뼈다발들, 하얀 머릿수건과 머릿수건에 엉킨
피묻은 머리칼을 조금 남겼네,
끝까지 웃던, 지하동굴을 울리던, 낮고 음습한
웃음소리

난 아르헨티나, 오월광장의 흰 머릿수건 두른 어머니들을
갑자기 기억했네,
80년, 5월, 광주, 무명인들의 묘와 실종자들,
이한열의 관을 뒤따랐던 무수한 만장,
화려한 만장이 산 자여, 따르라고
흐느끼는 것처럼 보였던,
다이아몬드 같은 아프리카의 검은 눈물,
내 아들을 쏘지 말아주세요 말하며
침략군의 탱크 앞을 맨몸으로 막아서던
체첸의 어머니들을,

fingers,
which covered her face,
and might have been the intense joy of an evil spirit
overflowing.

As the train approached casting an opaque light beam,
she threw her body down, falling
to the rails, where she died laughing.
Her life finished off by the weight of the train, she left
a pool of blood, a couple of piles of bones, a white kerchief
with a few strands of hair soaked with blood stuck to it.
Her laughter, that lasted till the end, ringing in the underground cave, was low and dark

I suddenly remembered:
mothers with white kerchiefs on their heads
in the Plaza de Mayo in Argentina.
May, 1980, in Kwang-joo. The anonymous graves and the missing.
The innumerable banners that followed the coffin of Yi Han-Yeol.
The brilliant banners seemed to sob, to urge the living to follow.

그리고 갑자기 웃음이 터졌어,
멈출 수 없는, 허파와 늑골을 울리는,
팔다리허리어깨를펼수없을정도로숨막히게터져나오는웃음소리
뉴욕, 지하철역을, 울리는 웃음소리는
인류의 밤에 대한 캄캄한 나의 답장, 헌사였는가

나의 웃음소리는 아주 오래된, 아주 넓은
영역에 걸쳐 있는 것이다,
숨쉴 희망이 부족하고 슬픈 희극, 엉터리 비극이
나날이 일어날 때
썰물의 물결 하나하나가 가진
상실, 박탈, 실종의 사연을 생각할 때 나는 웃는다,
연희동을 지나갈 때
여의도를 스쳐갈 때, 언론재벌사를 지나갈 때
나는 웃는다
나는 웃는다

검은 웃음, 석탄처럼 시커먼 절망에 짓이겨진,
까마귀 날개들의 대운하를 토하며
진폐증에 걸린 우리 시대의 폐로
나는 웃는다,
때묻은 광화문 이순신 장군 동상 옆에서

The black tears of Africa, like diamonds.
Don't shoot my son! The bare-handed mothers of Chechen
using their bodies to block
the invading enemy tanks.

And then suddenly I burst out laughing:
an unstoppable laughter that echoed in my lungs and against my
ribs;
a laughter that burst out, suffocating me and curling my arms
and legs, my waist and shoulders.
Is my laughter, echoing in the New York subway station,
my dark response, my dedication speech to the night of the
human race?

My laughter hangs over a very old, very wide realm.
When there is little hope of breathing, when tragic comedies
and fake tragedies occur daily:
When I think of the excuses for the losses, the brutal depriva-
tions, the missing,
at each wave of low tide, I laugh.
When I pass through Yonhee-Dong,
When I zip past Yeo-Eui-Do,

When I pass by the giant
media corporations,
I laugh and
I laugh:
Dark laughter, mashed against despair as dark as coal is black, vomiting up a great canal of crows' wings,
the lungs of our generation afflicted with black-lung disease.
I laugh
beside the grimy statue of Admiral Yi Soon-Shin at Kwang-Hwa-Moon.

솟구쳐 오르기 · 12

허우적대다
허우적대다
허우적대다
허우적대다
허우적대다

죽었는가
이젠 정말 죽었구나
했을 때
나는
떠
오
르
고
있었다

지상의 가장 끝에서
혼자 본
아침
해

백경의 장엄한 숨쉬기처럼

Soaring · 12

floundering
floundering
floundering
floundering
floundering

am I dead?
now I must really be dead
since I thought
i
f
l
o
a
t
ed
out

to the very edge of the earth
alone I saw
the morning
sun

물방울 분수를 조용히 내뿜으며
수면 위로
머리를 내밀어
고통의 신의 하사품을 받는 것처럼
고
요
하
게

가라앉는 행복조차 빼앗기고
아아, 또 살아났구나
휴우~~~하고 말하려는 것처럼
솟구치는
아
침
해
처
럼

like the majestic breathing of a great white whale
quietly spraying a fountain of water drops
and pushing its head
above the surface of the water
as if to receive gifts bestowed by the god of suffering
si
lent
ly

even the joy of sinking is taken away
ah! survived again
as if to say whew...
rising
morn
ing
sun

아네모네 꽃이 핀 날부터 · 1

죽도록 사랑하면
죽도록 사랑하면
그렇게 神氣가 오릅니까?

죽도록 사랑하면
죽도록 사랑하면
그토록 검은 질료에서 주황빛 신이 불려 나옵니까?

옛날부터 늘 그래 왔습니까?
목숨을 지나서도 타오르는
무슨 한 덩어리 불이 있겠습니까?

너무 모욕받았는데 너무 큰 모욕이 내려왔는데
울지 않아도 되겠습니까?

이렇게 괴로운데 이렇게 괴로워도
토막난 늑대의 이글거리는 횃불처럼
뭉쳐서 뭉쳐서 화려하게 꿈을 꿔도 되겠습니까?

From the Day the Anemone Bloomed · 1

If you love with all your heart,
if you love with all your heart—
does the divine spirit arise from this?

If you love with all your heart,
if you love with all your heart—
is the vermillion god called out from such black matter?

Has it always been this way from ancient times?
Is there a ball of fire
that burns beyond life?

Was it all right not to cry
when I was insulted by so great an insult that came down on me?

When I suffer like this—even if I suffer like this,
like the sizzling bonfire of a wolf hacked to pieces—
is it all right that our glorious dreams be
gathered together, gathered together?

아네모네 꽃이 핀 날부터 · 2

로프에 목을 걸고 다시 태어나야지,
그 뜨거운 동그라미밖에 다시 태어날 곳이
있어야지,
해도해도 못다 한 업고 속에서
가도가도 못다 간 수모 속에서

희망의 봉건주의 같은 것
난 정말 믿지 않아, 믿지 않지만

로프에 목을 걸고 다시 태어나야지,
그 붉은 동그라미밖에 다시 태어날 곳이
없으니까.

From the Day the Anemone Bloomed · 2

I must be reborn hanging on a rope by the neck.
I have no other place to be born but
in that hot noose.
In a world of inexhaustible penance
and on an unending journey of humiliation,

I certainly do not believe
such things as the preservation of hope. I do not believe, but

I shall be reborn hanging on a rope by the neck,
for there is nowhere else but in this red noose.

아네모네 꽃이 핀 날부터 · 3

—궁금해서 한번 전화해 봤어,
그래, 잘 지내? 잘 지내. 잘 지내!
이런 말도 통신인가?
이런 무책임한 것도 친구인가?
그래도 나는 수년의 침묵을 깨고
그녀에게 전화를 건다.

알코올 중독의 내 친구 니코틴 중독에
우울증 분열증 파라노이아
폐차장 가까운 데 서서
아이라인을 엉망으로 그리고 홀쌍꺼풀
짝짝이눈으로 웃고 있는
내 친구,
약 먹는 것이 내 유일한 취미야
그 증오하는 몸뚱이에 그래도 약까지 먹이고
무공해 사랑을 꿈꾸면서
우표처럼 어딘가로 날아가고 싶어하면서
(약은 무슨 약이니? 살충제야,
내 몸 속 벌레를 잡아야 해) 말하며 웃는

아침신문에, 보았니? 마리안 앤더슨이 죽었대
우리와 아무 상관이 없는 마리안 앤더슨

From the Day the Anemone Bloomed · 3

— I was just wondering...so I called.
Yeah, you're fine? I'm fine. I'm fine!
Is this communication?
Is this kind of irresponsibility friendship?
Nevertheless, I call her,
breaking the silence of a number of years.

My Friend, who is addicted to alcohol and nicotine,
and suffers from depression, schizophrenia, paranoia—
she stands near an automobile dump,
her eyeliner messed up,
and smiles with her eyes made uneven
by a single fold.
—Taking drugs is my only hobby.
Feeding her abominated body medicine,
she dreams of unpolluted love,
wishing to fly away somewhere like a postage stamp.
—(I am just kidding: there is no medication. Only pesticides.
I have to get rid of the bugs in my body.) She says this and
 laughs.
—Have you seen the morning paper? Marion Anderson died.
What's that got to do with us?

마리안 앤더슨과 아무 상관 없는 우리의
목소리가 갑자기 뚝, 하고 끊어지면서
두 여자의 떨어지는 몸무게 때문에
깊은 밤의 어둡고 둔중한 현이 텅, 하고 울린다.

우물의 밑바닥까지 떨어지기란 얼마나 어려운지,
먼지의 숨소리까지 다 들리는
메마른 우물의 맨 밑바닥에 던져져서
너와 나는,
(모친상 같은 흰 붕대를, 칭칭 동여감고)
왜 하늘의 별을 쳐다보았는지,
우물에 빠진 여자가 바라보는 저, 바깥,
하늘의 별만큼
목매달기 먼 것이 어디 있겠는가?

We having nothing to do with Marion Anderson, our voices
suddenly
jolt to a stop.
Taking the weight of our bodies as they fall, the dark, heavy
string of
the deep night resonates: plonk!

It's so difficult to fall all the way down to the bottom of the
well.
Thrown to the very bottom of the dry well
where the breath of a dust particle can be heard,
you and I—
(with white gauze bandages, like the deaths of our mothers,
wrapped around
us, layer after layer)
we looked up to the stars in the sky. Do you know why?
What could be further away
than the stars in the sky
for the women fallen into the well who gaze up,
wanting to hang themselves?

아네모네 꽃이 핀 날부터 · 4

우리들의 어머니는 하느님, 하느님 하고 새벽마다 기도를 한다.
트럭이 얼굴 위로 지나간 것 같은
으깨어진 흑인의 숙명. 백발이 성성한 검은 성모.
어머니들의 하느님은 트럭 운전사인가 보다.
엄마 때문에
엄마 때문에
저, 저, 저 매일 밥상이 엎어지는 어머니들의 숙명 때문에
우리는 하느님을 믿지 못한다.

고래는 어느 망망대해라 할지라도
작살에 꽂히면 반드시 그 작살이 꽂혔던 지점으로
되돌아간다고 한다.
살려고든, 죽으려고든.

엄마도 하느님도 바로 그 외경의 원리를
되풀이하고 있는지도 모른다.
그리고 아무래도 나도 나의 등을 애타게 만져본다.

몸이 나에게 괴로웠던 것은 옛날부터지만
아무래도 나의 등에도
아마 무슨 작살이 꽂혀 있는 것 같아서.

From the Day the Anemone Bloomed · 4

Our mothers pray to God, to God every morning.
The mashed fate of a black whose face
a truck has run over; a black madonna with graying hair.
Mothers' gods are truck drivers.
Because of moms,
Because of moms,
Because of the...the...the fate of moms whose tables are kicked
over
everyday,
we cannot believe in God.

Whales are known to return to the place
— no matter how deep the ocean—
where they were harpooned after they have been harpooned,
to live or to die.

Both Mom and God may be repeating that
principle of reverence.
And then, desperate, I try to touch my back.
My body has long been a pain to me,
but somehow, now, I feel a harpoon stuck
in my back, too.

콸, 콸, 콸, 피를 뿜는 작살이여,
우리는 아무도 자기 등을 완전히 만져볼 순 없지만
복받치는 피의 분수가
너울너울 타오르는 것을 느낄 때
나는 아득히 생각난다.
어떤 고통은 토착의 형식으로만 꽃피어난다고
하는 전설이.
그리고 나의 등에서 너울너울 꽃피어 타오르는
아네모네 둥근 뿌리의 찔러드는 파고듦을.

Pump, pump, pump: the harpoon spews out blood.
None of us can touch our backs everywhere,
but as I feel the surging fountain of blood
burn and flutter up,
I recall vaguely: a legend that
certain pain blossoms only where it is indigenous;
and also the boring down of the bulbous anemone root
into my back where flowers bloom and burn with dancing
flames.

날개의 파르티타~~~

비행기를 타려고 트랩을 올라갈 때
난 정말 음악적이 되는 거야,
구두를 벗고 강물에 뛰어들려는 사람처럼
어쩐지 이승을 한번 뒤돌아보고 싶은 사랑까지도
유쾌하게 느껴지지,
안녕~~~이라고 말해야 할 때만큼
무엇을 사랑하는 순간은 없는 것 같애.

이륙할 기점을 찾아
한없이 활주로를 선회하는 비행기 발목의 머뭇거림과
이륙할 때 부르릉거리는 비행기 모터의 진동력은
나의 팔목과 어깻죽지에 피 묻은 것을 느끼게 하네,
노스웨스트의 로고~~어떤 사람만이 어떻게 날아야
하는지를 안다~~~~~~라는 글귀를 읽었을 때
나는 왜인지 피냄새를,
비행기 가득한 피냄새를 느낄 수 있었어.

피냄새, 부르릉 부르릉 땅을 할퀴는 소리, 소리, 소리들에
나의 손톱에서 피는 철철 넘쳐흐르고
(지상을 떠나는 것이 그리 쉽지는 않겠지)
그녀가 이륙의 고통을 끝내는 금빛 날개를 활짝
펴고 고도를 찾으면 나도 내 몸을 구름 위로 활짝 펴

A Partita for Wings

When I go up the steps to board an airplane,
I truly turn musical.
Like someone taking off his shoes to leap into a river
and looking back in love once more at this life,
I even find it pleasant.
There is no moment when we feel a greater love
than when we say "Good-bye."

The hesitant ankles of the airplane
endlessly circling the runway
searching for a place to take off;
the roaring vibrations of the engine as the plane takes off
make me feel the blood in my wrists and shoulders.
When I read the Northwest slogan— "Only some people
know how to fly"— I can smell blood, for some reason:
the smell of blood permeating the plane.

The smell of blood, the roar as the plane crackles along the
 ground—vroom! vroom!—the noise, the noise…
blood flows from my fingernails.
(It can't be that easy to leave the earth!)
When the pain of departing from the earth has ended

구름의 흩어지는 무늬에
가볍게 몸을 실어버리지.

어린 시절 바람 속에 잃어버렸던 연을 찾아서
나는 가는 거라고 중얼거려,
나의 연과 친구의 연이 허공에서 만나
연줄과 연줄이 얽혔을 때
얽혀서 싸우다가 그만 나의 줄이 끊어져서
하늘 저, 너머에, 훨, 훨, 연을 잃어버리고
울면서 돌아오던 저녁길, 그때 만났던 어둡던
아버지의 영상도, 구름 속에 스치고

구름, 구름, 구름, 스침, 스침, 스침들……
스침보다 더 아름다운 만남이란 없는 것 같애,
비통한 할큄을 안 주고 무연하게 헤어지지 않니?
내가 매달렸던 것 나에게 매달렸던 것,
내가 묶여 있었던 것 나를 묶고 있었던 것,
내가 목매고 있었던 것 나를 목매고 있었던 것,
그런 것들을, 2만 8천 피트 고공,
구름 속 어딘가에 흩트려버리고
나는 환희에 차서, 피얼룩이 잔뜩 묻은 얼굴을 들고
미소하지,

and she spreads wide her golden wings to find her altitude,
I, too, spread open my body above the clouds
and let it glide across
the scattered pattern of the clouds.

I murmur to myself that I am going
in order to look for a kite I lost in the wind, in my childhood.
When my kite encountered my friend's in the void,
our lines got tangled,
and my line broke in the fight:
my kite flew away, fluttering across the sky.
That evening, on the road as I was going home full of tears,
I chanced to encounter my father
whose dark image
passed by in the clouds....

The clouds, the clouds, the clouds: all are brushing past,
  brushing, brushing....
There is none more beautiful than a passing encounter.
Do we not separate with no bad karma, with no painful
  scratches?
The things that I clung to and the things that clung to me;

땅의 역사를 기억하고 있는
나의 얼굴이 바람 속에 마구 구름을 타고 흩어지는 거야,
난 정말 말할 수 없이 쾌감을 느끼고
우린 정말 소멸을 향해 가는 존재로서
바람 속에 모든 상처를 묻어야 한다고
가볍게, 오, 희열에 차서
끄덕일 무렵이면

내려간다, 내려간다, 지금 착륙을 시도할 예정이오니
승객 여러분은 안전벨트를 묶고 자리에 앉아주시라고
한다,
내 몸은 내려가기가 싫어, 아 내려가기가 싫다고
울먹이고
아, 계속 날고 싶어~~~~~

뉴턴의 사과가 떨어졌던 힘을 따라서
음악은 꺼지고 비행기 바퀴는 무사히 땅바닥에 딱 닿는다.
모가지가 꺼억 하고 꺾이는 것 같고
나는 두 손에 피 묻은 날갯죽지를 들고 서서
어느 공항 대합실, 대형 거울 앞에서,
아직도 울고 서 있는 것만 같다.

the things that I bound and the things that bound me;
the things that I hung from and the things that hung from me:
I scatter all this somewhere in the clouds,
at an altitude of twenty-eight-thousand feet,
and, filled with joy, I smile holding up my face, which is
stained with blood.

My face, which recalls the history of the earth,
is wildly scattered in the wind as it rides the clouds.
I feel an indescribable pleasure.
Since we are headed for extinction,
we must bury all our wounds in the wind.
Gently, filled with ecstasy,
I begin to nod.... Just then:

Descent/descent. It goes down and down. As we are about to
attempt a landing:
Passengers! Please fasten your seat belts and remain in your
seats!
My body does not want to go down—No! I don't want to!—
and I break down crying.
O how I wish I could keep flying!....

Obeying the force that brought down Newton's apple,
the music stopped, the wheels of the plane touch down hard
on the ground,
and we are safe.
My neck breaks with a snap,
and I, the bloody wings in my hands,
seem to be standing
in some waiting room of an airport,
in front of a giant mirror,
still crying.

잔인한 편집

이디오피아 여인의 절벽 같은 검은 젖가슴에
매달려, 연필처럼 앙상한
이디오피아의 검은 아이가 죽고 있다,
죽고 있다,
소말리아의 자갈처럼 메마른 아이가,
사라예보의 귀신처럼 배고픈 아이가
(그 사진 바로 아래 이런 광고문)
날씬한 아름다움은 여인의 꿈이자 자존심,
아름다움은 절식으로 만들 수 있다,
절식을 위한 기적의 천연식물 엑기스, 다이어트 효모를 마시고
기적의 날씬한 미를.

나 원래는 그리 몰인정하고 무자비한 인간은 아니었다.
이런 편집의 틀 속에 오래 살다 보니
무자비한 망각의 학습이 계속 되었을 뿐, 뿐, 뿐.

Cruel Editing

Hanging on
to the sheer dark breast of an Ethiopian woman,
a dark child of Ethiopia, thin as a pencil, is dying,
...is dying:
a child as dry as a pebble in Somalia,
a child as hungry as a ghost in Sarajevo.
(Just underneath the picture reads an ad:)
Being slim and beautiful is the dream and pride of any woman.
Such beauty can be achieved by fasting:
drink the elixir of our miraculous natural herbs for fasting,
a yeast for dieting,
and become slim and beautiful by a miracle.

I was not such a cold and unsympathetic person in the
beginning.
It is just that, having lived so long in this framework of
editing,
I have merely—only merely—continued my study of cruel
oblivion.

왈, 가라사대

공자 왈, 맹자 왈,
예수 가라사대, 석가 가라사대,
석가 가라사대, 국가 가라사대……
태어나면서부터 우리는
왈과 가라사대의 시청자로 등록되었다,
특별입양 신청을 청원하지도 않았는데
태어나면서부터 우리는 기성복의 말 속에
입양되어 버렸다,
너답게 되기 위하여서라고,
입양된 아이는 당연히 세계 안에 편입됨으로써, 오히려, 자신이 되는
아이러니가 있다,

봄에 꽃이 피는 것을 보았니?
성냥갑을 켜다가
화상을 입고 맨살로 으깨진 열 손가락의 푸른 고통을
보았니? 거푸집이 내려찍힐 때의
국화빵 나신의 그 어머어마한 경련,
나, 나, 나, 나는……

꽃이여, 너 자신의 불로 꽉 들어찬,
너 자신의 흙의 血로, 너 자신의 흙의 肉으로,

Thus Has It Been Said, Thus Spoken

Confucius said. Mencius said.
Jesus spoke. Sakyamuni spoke.
Sakyamuni spoke. The Nation spoke....*
From our birth, we have been
enlisted as witnesses of "Thus they said" and "Thus they spoke."
Though we had never petitioned for adoption,
we were adopted at birth
into a world of readymade phrases.
In order to become more "you," the adopted child
ironically becomes more "himself" by being transferred
into the world of propriety.

Have you ever seen flowers bloom in the spring?
Have you ever seen the raw pain of ten fingers
burned and mangled beyond recognition
from having struck a match? The terrifying convulsion
of a naked waffle body** when the top half
of the waffle iron is lowered onto it.
I, I, I, I have....

As flowers filled with your own fire,
with your own blood from the earth, with your own flesh
from the earth,
with your own god from the earth,

너 자신의 흙의 신으로, 아무도 뺏을 수 없는
향기와 무늬로 활짝 꽃피어나는,
무슨 종교 이전의 원시신앙을
나는 사랑하노니,
너만의 운명의 형식이여, 향연이여

공자 왈, 맹자 왈
예수 가라사대, 석가 가라사대
석가 가라사대, 국가 가라사대……
나비채집이 가득히 들어 있는
희고 차가운 금속 손잡이가 달린
커다란 유리 진열장이 초능력의 왕릉처럼 떠오르고
떠오르다가, 둥둥, 떠다니다가,
내 머리에 와서 우르르 쾅 부딪치며 쏟아진다,
할! 방(棒)처럼 불현듯이 깨달음이 온다

이렇게 죽었다면 이런 죽음은
자연사인가, 의문사인가?
이렇게 산다면 계속 산다면
그런 삶의 제목은 자화상인가, 타화상인가?

I love primitive belief, over any religion,
which blooms with a fragrance and pattern
that no one can take away.
It is your own formal destiny, your celebration.

Confucius said. Mencius said.
Jesus spoke. Sakyamuni spoke....
Sakyamuni spoke. The Nation spoke....
A huge glass case filled with butterfly collections,
with cold, white metal handles,
rises up like a royal tomb
and bobs about
until it hits my head with a thundering roar
and collapses.
Aha! A sudden awakening hits me like a club!
If you die like this,
is the death from a natural cause or
is it suspicious?
If you live like this, or continue to live like this,
is your life a self-portrait, or a portrait by another?

---

* The Korean word for Sakyamuni" (or Buddha) is "Seok-ka" and for nation is "Kook-ka," the play of sounds obviously being lost in translation.

** "Waffles" here refer to the "Kook-hwa Pang" (lit. Chrysanthemum buns). They are quick-baked breads made in an iron mold and filled with sweetened red beans. The mold is shaped like chrysanthemum flowers and works like a waffle iron. Tr.

제도

아이는 하루종일 색칠공부 책을 칠한다.
나비도 있고 꽃도 있고 구름도 있고
강물도 있다.
　아이는 금 밖으로 자신의 색칠이 나갈까 봐 두려워한다.

누가 그 두려움을 가르쳤을까?
금 밖으로 나가선 안된다는 것을
그는 어떻게 알았을까?
　나비도 꽃도 구름도 강물도
　모두 색칠하는 선에 갇혀 있다.

엄마, 엄마. 크레파스가 금 밖으로
나가면 안되지? 그렇지?
아이의 상냥한 눈동자엔 겁이 흐른다.
　온순하고 우아한 나의 아이는
　책머리의 지시대로 종일 금 안에서만 칠한다.

내가 엄마만 아니라면
나, 이렇게, 말해버리겠어.
　금을 뭉개버려라. 랄라. 선 밖으로 북북 칠해라.
　나비도 강물도 구름도 꽃도 모두 폭발하는 것이다.
　살아 있는 것이다. 랄라.

Institutions

A child colors in his coloring book all day.
There are butterflies, flowers and clouds,
and also a river.
The child is afraid to color over the lines.

Who taught him this fear?
How did he come to know not to go over the lines?
The butterflies, the flowers, the clouds, and the river are all trapped
within the lines of the drawing.

Mommy, Mommy! The crayon shouldn't go over the lines, should it?
Fear flows across the tender eyes of the child.
My child, gentle and graceful, paints all day
keeping within the lines according to the instructions at the front of the book.

If I weren't his mom,
I would have said:
The hell with the lines! La, la-la! Paint right over the lines!
Butterflies, rivers, clouds, flowers—let them explode!

선 밖으로 꿈틀꿈틀 뭉게뭉게 꽃피어나는 것이다
위반하는 것이다. 범하는 것이다. 랄라

나 그토록 제도를 증오했건만
엄마는 제도다.
나를 묶었던 그것으로 너를 묶다니!
내가 그 여자이고 총독부다.
엄마를 죽여라! 랄라.

They are living! La, la-la!
Beyond the lines, wriggling and rising, they bloom.
They defy. They violate. La, la-la!

I have so despised institutions,
and yet Mom is an institution.
I am the Governor General!
To think that I bind you with the very thing
that bound me!
Death to Mom! La la-la!

모든 신발이 불편하다

모든 신발이 불편하다 나는 신발장을 연다
모든 신발이 가혹하다 나는 신발장을 닫는다

신발을 신고 나설 때마다 난 어떤 본능을 다치는
것만 같아, 골절, 뼈 뼈 뼈가 어긋 물린 것 같고 어떤 때는
도에 지나쳐 피 피 피가
길 위에 흘러내려 나의 길을 모가지로 감고 엉겨 저지하는 것 같아,
신발에서 길을 갈라내지 못하면
미친 듯이 신발의 길에 먹힐지도 모른다
신발에서 발을 추려내지 못하면
어쩌면 신발에서 발목을 잘라내야 할지도 모른다
거기다 또 신발의 중독에서 깨어난 발
발가죽의 중독에서 깨어난 뼈들조차
더 시끄러운 이 내란의 길목에 서서

꿈이여, 잠시 잠시만 더, 그래도, 이 가죽부대 같은 신발 안에
뭉쳐 있지 않겠니? 신발을 들고 날아가는 저 눈부신 태고의 날개가
하얀 자갈밭에서 알을 깨치고 날아가는
태양빛의 뜨거운 새처럼
고요히 중심의 원시신화 속으로 솟구쳐오를 때까지

All Shoes Are Uncomfortable

All shoes are uncomfortable. I open the shoe closet.
All shoes are cruel. I close the shoe closet.

Each time I put on my shoes and set out, I feel my instinct has been
 injured. My joints, my bones, bones and bones are all out of
 whack and at times my blood, my blood and blood spills onto
 the road where it wraps its neck around my way to stop me.
If I do not cut the road out of my shoes,
I might be insanely swallowed up by the road on my shoes.
If I do not salvage my feet from the shoes,
I may have to cut my ankles out of them.
Furthermore, as I stand at this street corner of the civil war,
my feet that woke from their addiction to shoes
and my bones that woke from their addiction to soles
make even more noise.

Dreams! Just for one more moment, won't you linger in these
 shoes, in these
leather sacs? Until those ancient wings of such blinding brilliance
carry the shoes and fly
like a hot bird in the sun,
until they break the egg on a white field of pebbles and fly away,

나의 발은 아직 할 일이 많고
나의 발은 아직 더 가고 싶은 길이 있단다

그리하여 엘칸토 금강 에스콰이어 비제바노 브랑누아를 넘어
레스모아 미스미스터 엘레강스 허쉬파피 랜드로바를 지나
갔습니다,
구두 大바겐에 가면 나에게 맞는 신발을 어쩌면 구할 수 있으리
라~
모든 신발이 뼈에 맞치고 근육은 구두에 대들고
발톱은 구두가죽을 찢고 한 발 가득 무성한 털은
솟구쳐 나와
한걸음 걸을 때마다
범주를 벗어난 모래와 엉긴 피가
나의 신발 너머 길 가득 수북히 넘치고 있으니

모든 신발이 수상하다 나는 신발장을 연다
모든 신발은 전족이다 나는 신발장을 닫는다

soaring silently into the midst of primordial mythologies,
my feet have much work to do
and still more roads to go.

So, passing by
El Canto, Keum-Kang, Esquire, Visevano, Blanc Noir, *
I went on,
past LessMore, MissMister, Elegance, Hush Puppies, Land Rover.*
Perhaps I would find shoes that fit me
if I went to a great bargain sale on shoes—
All the shoes struck my bones and my muscles protested;
my toenails tore at the leather and unruly hairs on my feet
poked through.
With each step I took,
blood, coagulated on the trampled sand,
overflowed onto the street past my shoes.

All shoes are suspect. I open the shoe closet.
All shoes are foot bindings. I close the shoe closet.

---

* Names of shoe stores in Seoul, Korea. Tr.

八福

의심하지 않는 사람은 복이 있나니
의심하지 않는 사람은 복이 있나니
의심하지 않는 사람은 복이 있나니
의심하지 않는 사람은 복이 있나니

땅의 나라가 저의 것이요

당연을 따르는 사람은 복이 있나니
당연을 따르는 사람은 복이 있나니
당연을 따르는 사람은 복이 있나니
당연을 따르는 사람은 복이 있나니

토끼장의 평화가 저의 것이라

Eight Blessings

Blessed are they who do not doubt.
Blessed are they who do not doubt.
Blessed are they who do not doubt.
Blessed are they who do not doubt.

For theirs is the kingdom of the earth.

Blessed are they who adhere to what is proper.
Blessed are they who adhere to what is proper.
Blessed are they who adhere to what is proper.
Blessed are they who adhere to what is proper.

For theirs is the peace of the rabbit hutch.

물새알 품은 산

산봉우리에 올라가보면
산봉우리보다 더 높은 것이
하늘 아래
우리 나라 산에는 많이 있지,

산봉우리 위에 올라앉은 봉분들은
어디보다 해를 많이 먹고
어디보다 바람이 많이 나서
푸르릉 푸르릉 금방이라도 금빛 깃을 떨치고
하늘로 날아 올라갈 듯하지,

봉분은 알처럼 따뜻하고
봉분은 물새알처럼 동그라서
해가 알맞고 바람도 알맞은 때가 되면
외로움 속에 기다렸던 그리움
이윽고 나른하게 천추의 알껍질은 깨어지고

물새 날개
깃을 치면서 훠이 훠어이
산을 넘고 물을 건너
머나먼 바다 그리운 어머니 계신 넓은 곳으로
날아가지

The Mountain with the Water Bird Eggs

If you climb to the top of a mountain peak,
there are many more things still higher
than the peak itself,
under the sky
in the mountains of our country.

The tumuli sitting atop the mountain peaks
receive more sun than anything else
and more winds arise from them than from anywhere else.
It seems they would fly up into the sky
at any moment, flapping their golden wings:
Flap! Flap!

The mounds are warm, like bird's eggs,
and they are round like the eggs of a water bird
when the sun is just right and likewise the wind;
longing lies waiting in loneliness;
the eggshell of a thousand years meekly breaks open.

The water bird,
flapping its wings slowly and freely,
flies

우리 나라 봉분은 무덤을 부화실로 만들고
산마다 가득가득한 산봉우리를 부화장으로 만들어
봄이 오면 이윽고 봄이 오면
물새알처럼 봉분은 부풀어
알은 깨어나고
하얀 물새알들은 날아가지 날아가지

갑자기 산은 텅 비고
보푸라기 보푸라기 금빛 새 깃들이
왜 산길마다 떨어져 있는지
텅 빈 산을 다른 알로 채우기 위해
이윽고 또 상여가 산으로 오네

over the mountains and river
to the far-away ocean, the wide-open place
where my mother is.

Our tumuli turn graves into incubators
and the mountain covered with mounds turns into an
  incubating field.
When spring comes, when spring comes at long last,
the mounds grow like water bird eggs
and the eggs hatch:
white water birds fly away, they fly far away.

Suddenly the mountain is empty
and fuzz balls of golden feathers
scatter over the mountain paths.
To fill the vacant mountain with new eggs,
yet another bier comes to it again.

결혼의 세계

—뉴욕의 희규에게

「결혼한 지 일 년이 되니까
이런 생각이 들어.
미혼의 세계는 FM 같고
기혼의 세계는 AM 같다고.
언니는 지금도 FM 방송을 더 많이 듣지?」

AIR MAIL 봉투를 뜯고
뉴욕 맨하튼에서 온 희규의 절망을 듣는다.
사실을 말하자면, 사실을 말해 버릴까, 사실을
말해 버릴 수 있을까, 난……
도무지 FM도 AM도 들을 시간이 없고
(나의 뇌에는 음악을 위한 자리도 상식을 위한
자리도 없기는 없다마는)
그보다도, 난, 스스로 AM 방송국이 되어
하루종일 상투적인 전파를 송신하고
퍼뜨리는 너절한 주부생활 방송국 국장이 되어

그런데, 희규에게.
「결혼한 여자라고 해서 FM을 안 듣는다는 건
잘못 유포된 미신이야. 결혼한 여자는 AM의 세계에만
머물렀으면 하는 건, 남자중심주의가 만든
민속신앙이야. 이상하지, 우리의 속신은 남자를 위해,

The World of Marriage

—To Hee-kyu in New York

"Now that I have been married for a year,
I think of things like this:
The singles world is like FM,
and married life is like AM.
Big Sister, you still listen to FM more, don't you?"

Opening the airmail envelope,
I listen to Hee-kyu's despair from Manhattan, New York.
To tell the truth, should I tell the truth? Can I tell
the truth? I ...
don't even have time to listen either to FM or AM
(I must admit that in my brain there is
no room for music or for common sense)
but I have turned into an AM station myself:
a shabby broadcasting director of the housewife's world,
transmitting and spreading banal radio waves all day long.

But, dear Hee-kyu,
"It is a mis-spread myth that a woman does not
listen to FM just because she is married. What
wants married women kept in the AM world
is a folk belief created by male chauvinists.

남자에 의해 만들어진 것이 더 많은데
여자들이 더 열렬하게 옹호하고 전파한다는 것은.
난 마음의 지하실에 무수한 FM 방송국을 세우고
떠 허물어. 물론 낮에는 AM 방송국에 근무도 하지.
다만 왼손과 오른손의 세계 어느 것 하나 잃어버리고
싶진 않아서.」

우리 집 마당귀에 서 있는 라일락 한 그루.
구름처럼 퍼져가는 보랏빛 향기.
저 불쌍한 땅을 데리고
향기의 초현실을 만드는 그녀를 닮기 위해
결혼의 세계엔 때로 살육과 뼈가 튀었다.

Isn't that strange? Our many gods are created for
and by men, but it is the women who protect and
propagate them more passionately.
I establish numerous FM stations in the cellar
of my heart and then destroy them. Of course,
during the day I also work at an AM station.
For I do not wish to lose either the world
of my left hand or the world of my right."

A lilac tree stands in the corner of our garden.
Its purple fragrance spreads like a cloud.
In order to emulate her who creates a surreal world
of fragrance on that pitiable plot of ground,
there were at times slaughter and bone cracking
in the world of my marriage.

두부 디자이너

이런 방식으로 존재하려고 했던 것은 아니었다,

원하지도 않는데 골다공증으로 뼈는 물렁물렁해지고
원하지도 않는데 살은 두부처럼 흐느적흐느적 무너지고
원하지도 않는데 원하지도 않는데
두부를 디자인하는 재단사들이 우리에겐 왜 이리
많은 것인가? 사정은 너도 마찬가지겠지만

두부 디자이너는 신문 속에도 있고
신문 뒤에도 있고
텔레비전 위에 텔레비전 속에 텔레비전 뒤에
제사상이 차려진 병풍 뒤에도 병풍 앞에도 병풍 속에도
잡다한 모임 혹은 태평양 건너의 어떤 곳
포크와 나이프
아니면 숟가락과 젓가락, 오오 모든 리모콘을 든 자들이
안 보이는 곳에서
새로운 통치의 디자인에 몰두하고 있는 것을
(두부 디자인보다 쉬운 일이 세상에 어디 있으리)

정말 이런 방식으로 존재하고 싶지는 않았다,
우리의 마음 밑에는 얼마나 많은 두부들이 경련하며
퍼들퍼들 쌓여 있는가,

Tofu Designer

I never intended to exist like this.

Though I never wanted it, my bones have become soft because
of osteoporosis.
Though I never wanted it, my flesh has collapsed and is as
limp as tofu.
Though I never wanted it, never wanted....
Why are there so many tofu cutters who design for us?
But you probably feel the same as I do....

Tofu designers are found in the newspapers,
and behind them;
they are above, within, and behind the television;
they are behind, before, and in the screen set out for our ancestral
memorial services;
and in a variety of miscellaneous gatherings, some perhaps
across the Pacific
with fork and knife
if not spoons and chopsticks. Oh, dear. All of them holding a
remote control
in some invisible place,
bent on coming up with the design of a new control

넋도 없고 뼈도 없이
오오 저 희끄무레한 면적으로만 존재하는
단지 면적으로만 존재하는
한모 두모 세모 네모의 두부, 頭部들

(what would be easier in this world to design than tofu?)

I never wanted to exist like this.

Within our hearts, how much tofu is heaped up,
wildly convulsing?
Having neither souls nor bones,
indeed existing as a whitish mass,
as only a block:
one, two, three, four squares of
tofu, heads.*

* "Tofu" is "tubu" in Korean. "Head" is also pronounced "tubu" and therefore there is a play on words. Tr.

토끼들의 시대

도시 한복판에서
애완용 토끼를 기르는 시대가 되었다,
죄없이 애완용 토끼 두 마리
높다란 아파트 베란다에 걸려 있어,
그것이 왜 꼭 종교적으로, 모욕적으로
보이는 나.

연분홍 토끼와 하얀 토끼
길고 하얀 두 귀가
쫑긋쫑긋 안테나처럼 빛나고 있어
—토끼를 애완용으로 기르다니 참 무서운.
—늑대를 길들여 집 개를 만든 것도 인간 아니야?
—온순하고 조용하고 또 예쁜
—가정적인 토끼, 창조적 불만족보다
순응적 온순함은 얼마나 좋은지

연분홍 토끼와 하얀 토끼
직업의 안정과 신분의 안정, 확실한 휴가의 보장
그 외에 무엇을 더 좋아해야 하는가?

퇴근길에 들르는 비디오숍
화장품 할인매장과 노래방들의 거리

The Age of Rabbits

It has now become an age to keep rabbits as pets,
right in the middle in the city.
The two innocent pet rabbits perched on the veranda
of a high-rise apartment building
seem to me,
in light of religion, only an affront.

A pale-pink bunny and a white one:
their long, white ears
wiggle and shine like antennas:
— Why would anyone keep bunnies as pets? What horrid....
— Wasn't it Man that tamed the wolf to be a domestic dog?
— Gentle, quiet, cute:
— familial rabbits. How much better to have obedient
  gentleness
than creative discontent.

The pale-pink bunny and the white one:
the security of job and status, the guarantee of a set vacation.
What else need one desire beyond that?
The video shop you stop at on your way home from work;
the streets filled with discount cosmetics shops and *karaoke*

무엇이 심각하게 더 슬플 것인가?
—일상성 속에 적멸보궁이 있다고 누군가
—뜨거운 진보는 옛 시대의 안개예요, 보세요,
집집마다 토끼들을 기르고 있잖아요
—누가 황토를 화살을 아침이슬을 다시 읽겠는가

베란다의 토끼들이 안방으로 들어가고
안방의 사람들이 베란다에 나와
토끼장 속으로 들어간다,
사람들이 토끼장을 가득 메우고
토끼들은 넥타이를 매고
회사로 백화점으로 거래처로도 가고
신용카드를 쓰고 사인도 하네
—행복에 이르는 기나긴 질병
—누군들 그 병에 걸리고 싶지 않겠는가
—야수적 창조성보다 행복한 순응이 더 좋아
언어의 위선들이여
일상성 속에 적멸보궁이
(그래도 밤새 들리는 철망 덜컹이는 소리)

club rooms—
truly, what could be more sad?
—Hasn't someone said that Nirvana is to be found among
the ordinary and mundane?
—Red-hot progress is the fog of olden times. Hey! Every
household has bunnies, hasn't it?
—Who will again read the yellow earth, the arrows, or the
morning dew?

The rabbits on the veranda go into the living room
and the people in the living room come out onto the veranda,
to the rabbit cage.
People fill the rabbit cages
and go off to their companies, their department stores, and
their places of business;
they use their credit cards and write their signatures.
—A chronic disease, striving for happiness:
—who doesn't want to catch it?
—Happy obedience is so much better than wild creativity.
Such hypocrisies of language.
In our mundane, everyday life,
there is Nirvana, Palace of Treasures.
(The chicken-wire cages still rattle all night long.)

비행기 납치

나 언젠가 비행기를 타면
미리 피스톨을 준비해 가야지
비행기가 이륙을 마치고도 한참 날아
아름다운 능금빛 허공 한복판쯤 이르렀을 때

나 호주머니에 피스톨을 감추고 몰래
기장실로 숨어들리라

그리고 죄없는 기장에게 총을 겨누고
준비해 온 유인물을 공손히 읽어야지,
—나 당신을 납치합니다. 정치적이거나 그런
이유는 결코 아닙니다, 단지 난, 난,
어느 곳에도 도착하고 싶지 않기 때문에,
〈이곳〉도 〈저곳〉도 아닌 허공, 하늘,
그곳에 계속 떠 있고 싶어서, 난, 난,
착륙하지 말고 계속 날아다니기만 할 것을, 명, 명,
명령합니다.

기장은 아마도 참 잘생긴 남자이리라.
그러나 어쩌겠는가,
내 마음은 무정부주의여서
어떤 〈여기〉에도 〈저기〉에도 속하기

Hijacking an Airplane

When, some day, I get to board an airplane,
I am going to take along a pistol.
When the plane has finished taking off and has flown quite
 some time
and reached the midst of a beautiful crabapple color,

I will slip into the captain's cabin,
the pistol concealed in my pocket.

I will point the gun at the innocent captain
and humbly read a printed page that I will have ready.
—I kidnap you, not for any political reasons or anything
like that, but because I do not want to arrive anywhere.
I want to keep gliding in midair, through the sky,
neither here nor there. So I, I com...com...
command you to keep flying and never land.

The captain would probably be a very handsome man.

But, what can you do?
My heart is an anarchist
and does not want to belong

싫은 것을,
아마도 그는 말하겠지
—하늘에서 연료가 떨어지면 추락하게 됩니다

추락? 공중폭발?
—상관없어요, 오, 그건 신경쓰지 않,

어느 허공 한복판에 산산이 흩어지는 연꽃이 될까
어느 바닷속에 침몰하여
하얀 고래에게 남김없이 뜯어먹혀
다시 어린 고래의 순수한 살이 되어
바람 속에 물푸레 무지개를 뿜어내는
장난 많은 어린 동물로 환생할까

내 마음은 무정부주의여서
〈여기〉도 〈저기〉도 아닌
어디 다른 곳에 있고 싶을 뿐,,,,,
,,,,그러니 어, 서, 비행기 한 대를 납, 치, 해, 야, 지,,,

either "here" or "there," wherever they may be.
He will probably say,
—If we run out of fuel, we'll crash.

Crash? Explode in midair?
—Doesn't matter. Don't worry about it....

Should I become a lotus blossom scattered everywhere in the
void,
or should I be eaten up, bit by bit, by a white whale
and become, in turn, true flesh of a young whale
and be reborn as a young playful animal
that spouts water in a rainbow of spray into the wind?

My heart is an anarchist
and wants only to be someplace else....
neither "here" nor "there."
....So I must hurry and hijack an airplane!....

『한국문학 영역총서』를 펴내며

한국문학을 본격적으로 번역하여 해외에 소개하는 일이 필요함을 우리는 오래 전부터 절실히 느껴 왔다. 그러나 좋은 번역을 만나기는 좋은 창작품을 만나는 것 못지 않게 어렵다. 운이 좋아서 좋은 번역이 있을 경우에는 또한 출판의 기회를 얻기가 쉽지 않다. 서구의 유수한 출판사들은 시장성을 앞세워 지명도가 높지 않은 한국의 문학작품을 출판하기를 꺼린다. 한국문학의 지명도가 높아지려면 먼저 훌륭하게 번역된 작품들이 세계적인 명성이 있는 출판사에서 출판이 되어 널리 보급이 되어야 하는데, 설혹 훌륭한 번역이 있다 하더라도 이 작품들이 해외에서 출판될 기회가 극히 제한되어 있어서, 지명도를 높일 길이 막막해지는 악순환을 거듭하는 것이 현실이다. 이런 현실을 타개하는 길은 좋은 작품을 제대로 번역하여 우리 손으로 책답게 출판하여 세계의 독자들에게 내놓은 데서 찾을 수밖에 없다. 이런 일을 하기 위해 도서출판 답게에서 『한국문학영역총서』를 세상에 내놓는다.

'답게' 영역총서는 한영 대역판으로 출판되며, 이 총서는 광범위한 독자층을 위하여 만들어진 것이다. 무엇보다도 이 총서를 통해 해외의 많은 문학 독자들이 한국문학을 알게 되기를 희망한다. 이 총서는 또한 국내에서 한국학을 공부하거나 영어로 번역된 한국 작품을 필요로 하는 영어 사용권의 모든 사람들과 한국문학의 전문적인 번역자들을 위한 것이기도 하다. 전문 번역인들은 동료 번역자들의 작업을 자신들의 것과 비교함으로써 보다 나은 새로운 번역 방법을 모색할 수 있을 것이다. 고급 영어를 배우기를 원하는 한국의 독자들도 대역판으로 출간되는 이 총서를 읽음으로써, 언어가 어떻게 문학적으로 신비롭게 또 절묘하게 쓰이는지를 깨닫는 등 많은 것을 얻을 수 있을 것이다.

아무리 말쑥하게 잘 만들어진 책이라도 그 내용이 신통치 않으면 결코 책다운 책일 수 없다는 자명한 이유에서, '답게' 영역총서는 좋은 작품을 골라 최선의 질로 번역한 책만을 출판할 것이다. 또한 새로운 번역자의 발굴과 격려가 이 총서 발간의 목적 가운데 하나이다. '답게' 출판사가 발행하는 이 총서가 한국문학 번역의 중요성을 다시 한 번 일깨우고, 문학 작품의 번역이라는 불가능한 꿈을 가능하게 하려는 번역자들의 노력에 보탬이 되기를 바란다. 이런 시도가 여러 가지로 유용하고 또 도전적인 것이 될 때, 더 나아가서는 잘 번역된 한국 작품의 전세계적인 출판 작업이 이루어지는 단초를 마련할 수 있을 때, 이 선구적인 계획은 진정으로 성공적인 것이 될 것이다.

김 영 무 (1944~2001)

Series Editor's Afterword

Extensive translation of Korean literature for foreign readers has for many years been felt to be a pressing need. But to fall upon a good translation is much harder than to discern a good original work. If we are fortunate enough to secure a good translation, it is often very difficult to get it published abroad.

The major publishers of the western world are not yet prepared to run the risk of publishing works of relatively unknown Korean literature. Yet if Korean literature is to achieve worldwide fame, it first of all needs to be well translated, and then put into circulation throughout the world by those very publishers which are so reluctant to publish even good translations of Korean literature. It is a vicious circle: no publication without fame but no fame without publication. To save the situation, we should perhaps try to make available to readers abroad choice translations we ourselves have published in editions of high quality. The DapGae English Translations of Korean Literature series has been launched with this aim.

Each volume of the DapGae series will be a bilingual edition. We expect a wide-ranging audience for the series. It is our primary hope that it will help introduce many foreign readers to the world of Korean literature. The series is especially intended to serve English-speaking students enrolled in Korean literature courses, as well as those who may wish to compare their own translations with the translations of fellow translators in order to find new and better ways of translating. Korean readers studying advanced English can also benefit from reading these bilingual editions: the experience may help them to recognize the mystery of true mastery of the literary use of language.

However well designed a book may be, it cannot properly serve its purpose if the contents are mediocre. For that reason the DapGae series will strive to introduce to the readers of the world the best translations of the finest works of Korean literature. One of the objectives of the series is to find and encourage new talents in English translation. We hope that the DapGae English Translations of Korean Literature series will serve in some small way to refocus attention upon the importance of translating Korean literature into good English and to make possible the impossible dream of literary translation. This pioneering project will be a true success not only if it proves useful and challenging but also if it paves the way for the publication of fine translations of Korean literature on a worldwide scale.

Young-Moo Kim (1944~2001)

저자와
협의하여
인지 생략

달걀 속의 生

지은이 | 김 승 희
펴낸이 | 東原 張少任
펴낸곳 | 도서출판 답게

초판 인쇄 | 2007년 3월 15일
초판 발행 | 2007년 3월 20일

등 록 | 1990년 2월 28일, 제 21-140호
주 소 | 143-838 서울시 광진구 군자동 469-10호(2F)
전 화 | (편집) 02)469-0464 · (영업) 02)463-0464, 02)498-0464
팩 스 | 02)594-0464
홈페이지 | www.dapgae.co.kr
e-mail | dapgae@chollian.net, dapgae@korea.com

ISBN 978-89-7574-221-7

ⓒ 2007, 김승희(원작)
ⓒ 2007, 김경년(번역)

나답게 · 우리답게 · 책답게

* 책값은 뒤표지에 있습니다.
* 잘못 만들어진 책은 구입하신 서점에서 교환해 드립니다.

역자 소개

김경년 & Steffen F. Richards

김경년은 시인, 교수로 U. C.버클리에서 한국어와 번역을 강의하고 있다. 남편인 스테픈 리챠즈는 U. C. 버클리에서 동아시아 문학 전공으로 석사학위를 받았으며, 일본문학을 영어로 번역하기도 했다. 또한 시인으로서 Light, Dark Wind, Moon (Aventine Press, 2004)시를 발표했다.

두 사람은 윤동주 시전집, 김승희 시선집, 윤후명 소설 "둔황의 사랑"을 영역하였으며 강은교, 황동규 시 등을 번역하기도 했다. 김경년은 1.5 세 한인 작가로 요절한 차학경의 "딕테"를 한국어로 번역 출간 하기도 했다.(토마토출판사 1997, 어문각 2004)

시인으로서 김경년은 "심상", "샌프란시스코 문학지", "샌프란시스코 펜문학", The Seventh Quarry (Swansea Wales) 등에 한국어 시와 영문시 등을 발표했으며 샌프란시스코 판 한국일보와 중앙일보에도 시와 수필을 발표하고 있다.

두 사람은 번역가로서 한국문학번역원과 문예진흥재단의 번역 지원을 받았으며, 김경년은 코리아타임즈의 번역문학상(시부문 최우수, 1996), 한글발전 공로로 대한민국국무총리표창(2004), 국제펜클럽 번역문학상(2006) 등을 수상한 바 있다.

The Translator

Kyung-nyun Kim Richards is a poet and lecturer at U.C. Berkeley, where she teaches the Korean language. Steffen F. Richards, her husband, has a Master' s Degree in Oriental Languages from U.C. Berkeley and a background in translating from the Japanese also a poet, he is a contributor to Light, Dark Wind, Moon (Aventine Press, 2004.) Together, they have translated works by Yoon Dong-joo (Asian Humanities Press, 2003), Kim Seung-hee (Homa & Sekey Publishers, 2004), Yun Humyong (Cross-Cultural Communications, 2005) and Kang Eun-kyo. Her translation of Theresa Hak-kyung *Cha's Dictee* into Korean, which was first published in 1997, was republished in 2004 by Omungak Publishers, Inc. in Seoul, Korea. Her original works have appeared in *Shim-sang(Poetry: Image and Criticism)*, *San Francisco Moon-hak-ji* (Literary Journals), San Francisco PEN Literature, The Seventh Quarry (Swansea, Wales). She contributes poems and essays to The Korea Daily (JoongAng Ilbo Daily) and The Korea Times Daily (HanGook Ilbo Daily), both San Francisco Editions. They have been recipients of grants from the Korean Culture and Arts Foundation, 1997-1998, the Korean Literature Translation Foundation, 1998-1999, and the Korean Literature Translation Institute, 2004-5.

Kyung-nyun Kim Richards was the top prize winner of the Literature Translation Contest held by the Korea Times of Republic of Korea, 1996 and the recipient of a Commendation of the Prime Minister of Republic of Korea for her contribution to the translation of Korean literature, 2004 and PEN (Korea) Translation Award 2006.